Alpha Therapy-Targeting (AT-T)

William P. Macklin, M.A.

PublishAmerica
Baltimore

ISBN: 1-4137-6684-6
PUBLISHED BY
PUBLISHAMERICA, LLLP.
www.publishamerica.com
Baltimore

Printed in the United States of America

To all of you who trusted me and my AT-T enough to tell me about your secret fears; to those of you who kept telling me I should write this book; to my family for encouraging me, and for putting up with my occasional obsession with the book project; to my wife, Karen, who rescued me at the last minute by showing me how to make the new computer do things I needed it to do; and to my daughter, Saivani, the gifted violinist, for insisting I do it right: I dedicate this book. Thank you all. And I thank God—whoever He, She or It may be.

Acknowledgements

I realized years ago that most mainstream psychology books are not very good sources of useful information about psychology or psychotherapy. This is because they are too reflective of American cultural values, and not sufficiently reflective of accurate information regarding what is truly known, what is just assumed and what is still not understood about human psychology, regardless of cultural context. Since then I have read many books that would probably make most psychotherapists shake their heads, wondering at my interest in such seemingly irrelevant topics. I've lost track of the many authors on all kinds of subjects—some not even about psychology, per se—who have influenced my thinking and guided my insights into the demystification of human psychology. In addition to hundreds of clients and thousands of AT-T therapy sessions, I am doubtless indebted to a great many authors who wrote on a very wide range of subjects.

When I was sent by my onetime employer, a California prison, to a training given by that old half hippie-half Buddhist genius Ken Keyes in Carmel, California, I was about to find out how psychotherapy really works. Ken is dead now, but his training and his books influenced me to change from a standard talk therapist into an effective psychotherapist. I'll never forget his words on the telephone, "This—Ken's system—doesn't belong to me, Bill, it belongs to God." This was followed by his written permission to develop and to expand on what I had learned from him in any way I saw fit, as long as it helped people.

Ken and I had poliomyelitis in common. Mine was very mild compared to his. But years later I experienced what is called post-polio syndrome, and I gradually lost the ability to walk. After some surgery and a lot of physical therapy I regained the ability, although I still walk rather like a drunk. Meanwhile, I was unable to work, so I passed the time at my computer, debriefing myself, as it were, of all I knew about psychology, psychotherapy and the human emotions, mind, body and spirit in general.

After about two years of doing this I realized I knew—and could explain—quite a lot about psychology and psychotherapy that isn't found in mainstream books, or is explained incorrectly. For years clients of all kinds and all ages had been telling me I should write a book about AT-T. My answer was usually that I'm a psychotherapist, not a writer of books. Gradually, though, during my treatment and convalescence I realized I had written the book—just to pass the time—and all it needed was to be organized into book format.

As the reader goes from paragraph to paragraph, it will be noted that sometimes I use the term "you," as if I am directly addressing the reader. Perhaps in the very next paragraph I use the depersonalized term "one," to make a more generalized point. In yet another paragraph I use the term "client," in which case I am trying to grab the attention of the reader who is a psychotherapist. I hope these sudden changes do not cause too much confusion. As I read and re-read the manuscript, it always seemed necessary to make such changes.

Much of the material in this book is repetitive; the same facts sometimes re-appear, but in a slightly different context. This too I considered necessary, largely because human psychology is a rather complex, immeasurable subject. While avoiding technical terms as much as possible, I tried to make it clear what AT-T is and what it is not.

I owe a great debt of gratitude to two people who were incredibly helpful in formulating AT-T into a book that became worth publishing, worth buying and worth reading, and more importantly, worth using to neutralize fear triggers. The first one is my daughter, Saivani Sonali Macklin. My wife and I adopted her as an infant from Calcutta, India. At about age 17 or 18, she looked me in the eye in that wise way she often has, and said, "Dad, take out all the big words and write it so people can understand what you're saying!"

She was right, of course. She knows I tend to go a little overboard when it comes to using just the right word, often making a point so technically precise that sometimes I'm the only one who understands what I'm trying to say. So, I re-wrote the entire book! Sure enough, I liked it better the way she had suggested!

The second person to whom I am incredibly indebted is Melisa Finch, Ph.D., a licensed clinical psychologist. She was a psychotherapist at an Arizona Juvenile Corrections facility, as was I. I never got to know her very well because we were always too busy. But I noticed most authors had someone proofread their manuscripts, so I asked her to proofread mine. She said, "They didn't call me the 'graduate school queen of proofreading' for nothing!" She went over my manuscript with utter brutality—and it needed it. I had no idea I could make so many mistakes and not catch them myself. Bless her, bless her, bless her! Thank you, Queen Melisa.

Biographical Sketch

Macklin lived at Folsom, San Quentin, Soledad, and Walla Walla prisons, where his father worked. Macklin had the second highest IQ in his college; earned a B.A. and an M.A. in psychology; was a therapist in several other California prisons; a court investigator; a counterintelligence agent in the U.S. Army; and a therapist for the Arizona Department of Juvenile Corrections.

Table of Contents

Introduction

The THERAPEUTIC INTERVENTION DESCRIBED IN this book will eventually change the way most psychotherapy and most counseling is done! It describes a surprisingly simple way to permanently disconnect a client's (or the reader's) Fight-or-Flight emotions from whatever triggers them. It explains how social and self-esteem "fear triggers" are what cause all the various kinds of fear feelings: *nervousness, worry, boredom, anxiety, hurt, sadness, guilt, shame, envy, panic, horror, disappointment, terror, and especially embarrassment.*

There are no anger triggers as such. Anger is a "defense mechanism," whether in the form of mild annoyance or more severely in the form of rage or hate. Anger arises in response to a threat to one's ego; that is, one's sense of self-esteem or one's sense of social status. Put simply, an anger problem is in reality a fear problem. The function of the anger defense mechanism in humans (and likely in animals) is to defend against the threat represented by a fear trigger. When there is no fear, there is no anger!

If you can recognize enough of your fear feelings, identify

what or who triggers them, perform the self-administered technique described in this book on each one, your anger, your resentment, your stunted maturity, interference with your natural intelligence, your avoidance of reasonable challenges in life, phobias, etc., will be gone! That is the substance of this book.

As a human you have little, if any, real need for the anger and fear emotions of your Fight-or-Flight (F-or-F) instinct—which should have been called the Flight-or-Fight instinct, since anger is always preceded by the threat of a fear trigger. It is referred to as an instinct because we were born with it and because it is so evident in animals. The fear/anger response in wild animals usually occurs when there is a direct physical threat, when another animal comes between a female and her offspring, when another animal interferes with an animal's access to food, and sometimes relative to mating competition, territorial conflict, and some other oddities. This is seldom the case with humans. The human F-or-F emotional responses are triggered by whatever seems to pose a threat to self-esteem and/or social status in one form or another.

It is quite clear that your fear and anger emotional reactions to self-esteem and/or social status threats are not your best resource. In fact, every person knows from observing others as well as from personal experience that fear in any of its forms and anger in any degree of intensity usually make things worse. For one thing, fear and anger lower your functional intelligence.

You have a great variety of more dependable and more effective resources for resolving problems and for getting your needs met. These include, but are not limited to, abstract thinking, tolerance of ambiguity, patience, forgiveness, insight, explanation, altruism, compassion, spiritual reference, and the list goes on and on. Individually and collectively these uniquely human resources are infinitely more effective than your fear and anger, regardless of the situation, emergency, crisis or any of life's challenges.

Yet most people, even many psychotherapists, do not realize there is always a connection between fear and anger. There are some who do not even believe it! It is not taught in schools. It receives only passing reference in most religions. In fact, most everyone—with certain exceptions which will be discussed later—even many psychotherapists (!), still believes fear and anger are a necessary part of being a normal and healthy person. Chances are you, the reader, still believe in this myth!

Every person, family, peer group, political party, culture, and so on, has beliefs as to when and why it is acceptable for a person to feel afraid. Each also has expectations as to when and why a person ought to be angry! In addition, there are even expectations as to how fear and anger can be acceptably displayed or acted out. The whole idea of placing positive value on either fear or anger is *patently absurd*, as will become quite clear later in this book.

In the everyday business of managing subordinates, whether in social "pecking order" or in corporate ranks, and maintaining self-esteem—or self-respect, as some call it—anger is oddly thought of as a helpful emotion! This is probably because it tends to hide one's fear feelings from others and from oneself. Until now there has been no easy and reliable way to rid ourselves of our fear or anger reactions to whoever or whatever triggers them.

Cognitive therapies continue to be the primary vehicle for dealing "therapeutically" with people who have anger problems. Anger Management, whether it be Reality Therapy (Glasser), Transactional Analysis (Berne), Behavior Modification (Wolpe, Skinner), Gestalt Therapy (Perls), Rational Emotive Therapy (Ellis), Client Centered Therapy (Rogers), Paradoxical Therapy (Haley; Rabkin), and others, are fundamentally cognitive methodologies.

AT-T is a radical departure from cognitive therapies. As such, it will not initially be well received by those therapists who still believe in these one-size-fits-all cognitive methodologies. There will always be a need for cognitive training for individuals who were reared in family environments that lacked pro-social role models. But cognitive therapies do little or nothing of a lasting nature about the fear and anger feelings that reinforce negative and/or self-defeating behaviors and attitudes. AT-T fills this gap in the current treatment of behavior and emotional problems.

Virtually everyone has experienced an angry parent during early childhood. They have thereby been neurologically imprinted with a fear-motivated respect for displays of anger. This is probably why so many people tend to have a fearful respect for such displays.

Fear (Flight) emotions make you feel powerless, vulnerable, socially isolated, incompetent, stupid, clumsy, and so on. Did Sir Winston Churchill have an inkling when he made his famous statement, "the only thing we have to fear is fear itself"? Fear emotions are true "victim" emotions, and for that reason they are the most unpleasant to experience.

The anger defense mechanism is not activated every time one is confronted with what seems a fear trigger. Cultures, subcultures, families, social groups, and so on, all have unwritten rules governing when it's okay to display fear feelings or anger feelings and when it's not okay, as well as how one should display them. Some examples of allowable display of fear are: death of a loved one; death of a favorite pet (sometimes); dire physical threat; performing musically (sometimes); etc. Some examples of allowable display of anger are: being insulted in front of an audience of peers; an insult to your family; an insult to your race; an insulting comment about your favorite political candidate; etc. Such rules are the reason why people so often pretend they are unafraid, or deny being afraid even when their fear is obviously visible to others. This predicament is experienced from time to time by virtually everyone.

Do you routinely try to avoid people or situations that make you feel uncomfortable? Of course you do! The *mere anticipation* of a potential threat to self-esteem or social status is a fear trigger, rather like an emotional early warning system. You generally "defend" yourself from these threats internally via anger-based thinking, such as avoidance justified by disapproval, criticism, fault finding, etc., or externally by overt angry acting out, verbally and/or physically.

Most all people and cultures generally disapprove of public displays of fear. Each of us learned this first at home, then in the neighborhood, then in school, and finally as an adult on the job. You are supposed to "suck it up," meaning hide it. It seems most people disapprove of a whiner or a complainer or a crybaby or a whistle-blower.

When your anger defense mechanism is activated, it is almost instantaneous. It is doubtful that becoming afraid or angry are conscious choices. Even mild anger, like impatience or annoyance or boredom, tend to occur as if on auto pilot. Each person has a learned—early childhood conditioning—repertoire of degrees and forms of fear and anger which are activated, without conscious intent, in response to certain fear triggers. While there are similarities among people and among cultures, each person in each culture is somewhat unique in regard to what they learned to experience as fear triggers. They also learn—early childhood conditioning—which fear triggers warrant a fear response only and which ones also warrant the anger defense mechanism response.

You try not to think about your fear triggers, preferring to think of yourself as being relatively fearless. Having observed from childhood through adulthood that the public display of fear feelings is generally frowned upon, you have invented supposedly non-fear-related—but anger-based—reasons to avoid situations and people who pose a fear threat. As already mentioned, these consist of criticism, disapproval, resentment, blaming and various other forms of anger-based thinking and judging.

The devaluing of people or situations perceived as potential fear triggers is an anger-based response, regardless of how mildly or how intellectually or even how accurately they are expressed. One's anger defense mechanism can occur so quickly and automatically that one is often unaware it was a fear threat that triggered it. One's anger defense mechanism "protects" one from one's own fear feelings by enabling the mental judgement of the other person or situation as "wrong" and oneself as "right."

You will realize, once you give it some thought, that you seldom recognize your criticism, disapproval, resentment, blaming, and so on, as anger-based, or that your anger is fear-based. Simply put, anger feels better than fear. You learned as a child, by watching adults, to think of your anger as a form of self-protection in many situations and with certain people. By now your personal style of anger is so habituated that it no longer requires a thought process. You just accept it, and you blame the person or situation that supposedly is "responsible" for it.

There are some rather odd exceptions to the "suck it up" rule. One is the wider latitude supposedly allowed women for the display of certain fear emotions. But what a price they pay for a little freedom of emotional expression! Because of it they are considered too emotional and too sentimental. Most males have learned to cover up and to be in denial of their fear emotions—and even many females!—and consider most women intellectually limited because of what is considered their "excessive sensitivity."

The main obstacle to successful therapy is your basic instinct to seek pleasure and to avoid pain, whether physical or emotional. This instinct is an important human asset, but only when you learn to use it in a manner more appropriate for humans. Humans need to learn that being truly fearless, and therefore virtually free of anger, is pleasure, and that pretending to be fearless and having to rely on the anger defense mechanism is pain. Then the pleasure/pain principle serves as a guide for the identification and neutralization of fear triggers, thus reducing the need for anger.

Unfortunately, most of us learned to use the pleasure/pain instinct to protect ourselves from self-esteem fears and social status fears and from the people and situations that threaten to trigger them. For this reason it can be difficult for a person to recognize that fear lurks behind their angry talk and/or angry acting out, as well as their anger-based—which is fear-based—resentment, mental criticisms, disapproval, etc. As already mentioned, anger makes us feel "right" and enables us to confidently believe it is someone else's or something else's fault that we feel angry. For a fear trigger to be resolved, however, it must first be identified. In the case of the anger defense mechanism it most often requires the assistance of a therapist who knows how to guide the client in recognizing the fear triggers behind the anger.

Until the appearance of Alpha Therapy-Targeting—and EMDR, developed by Francine Shapiro, Ph.D., when and if it is used in this manner—there has been no easy and reliable way to permanently neutralize fear triggers. In the Western world current psychotherapy is primarily cognitive. Perhaps the presenting problem is analyzed and defined and the client comes to realize how the problem came about, including how they might have contributed to the problem. Then the client is guided in ways to rethink the problem more effectively and to react to it more appropriately. This can be adequate treatment if a client's problems are not strongly reinforced by fear, or the fear is not too strongly defended by anger. But, if the client continues to rely on the anger defense mechanism and its associated justifications, the benefits of cognitive therapy are usually short term, if there are any benefits.

This fundamental description applies to Gestalt Therapy, Dialectical Behavior Training, Reality Therapy, Encounter Group, Transactional Analysis, Behavior Modification—which usually has little effect if the client is over 10 years old and is aware that Behavior Modification is being attempted—and so on. The sessions begin somewhat as teacher-student, and hopefully evolve into a kind of "meeting of the minds" between therapist and client. Fear and anger emotions are addressed, but only intellectually.

While the above description of cognitive psychotherapy might seem unfairly oversimplified or even seem trivialized, it is done only to make a point about the unique approach and outcome expectations of Alpha Therapy-Targeting. AT-T approaches a problem quite differently. It addresses fear triggers exclusively, and in so doing it renders the anger defense mechanism unnecessary as far as those fear triggers are concerned, even if and when they re-occur. This frees up the client's higher intellectual levels to the extent that they were being interfered with by fear and/or anger emotions. This is definitely nontraditional!

A client, however hopeful for emotional relief, will have

doubts that any lasting good will come out of any kind of therapy session. They bring mixed feelings of hope and despair. It is unlikely there is any neurological imprinting from early childhood that would provide a basis for them to expect a truly rewarding outcome from psychotherapy. But after applying the AT-T intervention to several fear triggers a client will realize fairly soon how incredibly amenable they are to truly satisfying emotional change. As a result of these early successes, the client begins to consider disclosing some of their deepest, darkest secret fears so they can be resolved via the AT-T therapeutic intervention.

The reader might now begin to re-consider the pleasure/pain instinct and begin to see how it could be functioning far more beneficially on a higher, more human level. Although resentment undeniably feels better than fear, the AT-T client gradually discovers that calm self-confidence feels a lot better than resentment, blaming, or any other anger-based defense mechanism! AT-T teaches the client to use the pleasure/pain principle as a human resource, rather than just animal instinct.

AT-T enables the client, or the reader who self-applies AT-T, to experience calmness, self-confidence and more reasonable thought patterns and behaviors as *pleasurable*; fear-based and anger-based emotions, thought patterns and behaviors become recognized as *unpleasant* and at times emotionally and physically *painful*. This is a uniquely different perspective on life, and can have only a beneficial impact on one's spiritual life as well as on one's emotional life.

Eventually many clients will no longer need the continuing support and maintenance of the Alpha psychotherapist. The AT-T therapeutic intervention is so simple, once some clients understand it, perhaps with a few guided sessions, it can be self-applied without requiring the presence of a psychotherapist. In fact, a secondary goal of the AT-T psychotherapist is to eventually enable some clients to become their own therapist. For this reason, although not its primary intent, AT-T sometimes turns out to be what is called "short-term therapy."

The State of the Art—Science!

We do a disservice to psychology by referring to it as an art. It is not an art. It is a science. The methods and techniques of psychotherapy—the ones that work!—can be analyzed, defined and explained, tested and replicated, just as with any other science.

About five years into my profession as a therapist it occurred to me that if I had a serious emotional problem I would hesitate to seek help from someone like me. I was practicing some of the mainstream therapy methods and techniques of that time. Yet, I was rarely able to predict outcome. Although most of my clients seemed to benefit from my services, I was seldom able to identify exactly what I had done that had produced those benefits. I began asking other therapists to tell me what worked best in their practices. This was a disappointing survey. They all had something to say about client resistance, but none of them could give me a coherent explanation of what specific technique worked best and why it worked.

Many said they were "eclectic," which at first sounded rather learned, as if they had mastered a variety of effective techniques. But none could describe any specific technique or methodology they could count on. Many had adopted a "favorite" system, such as Gestalt Therapy, Transactional Analysis, Encounter Group, Dialectical Behavior Training, Behavior Modification, Reality Therapy, etc. But, however admirable in theory and design, they are all cognitive therapy systems…reinventions of the same wheel. It seems to be a cultural belief system that most emotional, behavioral and psychological problems could be resolved if only clients would just learn to think more clearly…use better reasoning skills.

This is not to say therapists then and now fail to help their clients. In fact, quite the contrary. All of these systems, and the therapists who apply them, can lay legitimate claim to benefiting most of their clients to some degree. But their "failures" were invariably attributed to "client resistance." There was, and still is, a lot of "art" and little or no science in the general practice of psychotherapy. Unable to scientifically defend their favorite methodology, many psychotherapists engaged in fierce verbal attacks on each other's theories. Many still do!

It was discouraging to think that my effectiveness as a trained psychotherapist might be due primarily to the quality time I spent listening nonjudgmentally to my clients. It was troubling to consider that some of my carefully administered techniques might actually have been irrelevant. What if the benefits realized by some of my clients were no more attributable to my skills than to the color of my necktie?

I have met with quite a few psychotherapists, clinical directors and program managers over the past few decades. To this day it is only a rare few who ever asked me what therapeutic interventions I have found the most reliable or the most beneficial to my clients. There seems to be a polite understanding that therapists shouldn't embarrass one another by asking for a definitive explanation of what they do for their clients and, more importantly, how and why it works. Whenever I have asked recently educated clinicians what methodologies they most rely on, every one has said cognitive therapy! It seems today's colleges and universities turn out psychotherapists who diagnose their clients, and then try to teach them a better way to think about what is troubling them.

Whenever I have described the quite impressive benefits of Alpha Therapy-Targeting to my colleagues, they usually seem not at all interested! I believe they think I am exaggerating. After all, most of the more well-known therapy systems started out in an atmosphere of great expectations and enthusiastic marketing, usually generated by a therapist with charisma, some endearing personal qualities, or some very good marketing skills. The practitioners of those systems are still providing services and they are still training new therapists, but their techniques no longer stand out as the breakthrough systems they were once thought to be.

The system of Eye Movement Desensitization and

Reprocessing (EMDR) developed by Francine Shapiro is uniquely different. It can be learned and replicated by any competent psychotherapist. The quality of outcome is highly predictable and the time frame is virtually immediate! Some therapists are doing their best to explain why EMDR doesn't really work, but their criticisms seem anemic in the face of all the predictable therapeutic successes of EMDR. Many psychotherapists, let alone clients, just cannot believe psychotherapy can be that easy! The reason why EMDR works so well will become apparent to the reader as the function of Alpha brain waves in AT-T is explained.

Alpha brain waves are usually associated with pre-sleep drowsiness, post-sleep grogginess or just daydreaming. Such mental states are generally considered unproductive, a waste of time…but sometimes restful. More accurately, it is likely Alpha brain waves play a major role in our lives by creating the mental—neurological—environment for higher functioning in all our endeavors, from sports performance to creative thinking to insight development.

There is a great deal of clinical research being conducted in many countries regarding brain wave interaction. It will not be long before this research explains when and why psychotherapy is effective, as well as when and why it sometimes is not effective. But the understanding of Beta and Alpha brain wave interaction in psychotherapy is the means by which psychology is becoming ready to join the other sciences.

Shapiro's EMDR seems to be a major step in the direction of a science of psychotherapy. When done correctly, it works every time! Alpha Therapy-Targeting can be considered the next step for at least two reasons: First, AT-T focuses on the strategic induction of Alpha brain waves instead of on the significance of eye movement back and forth and the unclear theoretical relationship to problem solving during rapid eye movement (REM) sleep. Second, AT-T works just as well on relatively minor, or even seemingly trivial, stress situations as it does on post-traumatic stress disorder (PTSD).

In fact, in the body of this book it will become clear that all of one's fears and angers are fundamentally PTSD issues. Targeting introduces a new perception of PTSD: *all self-esteem, emotional and behavioral problems not neurologically based—via genetics, injury, substance abuse or disease—are fundamentally the equivalent of PTSD.*

Primal Therapy, introduced by Arthur Janov, is another system that relies on repetition—and therefore an increase in Alpha brain waves. Since it does not take brain waves into consideration, it is possible that the few individuals who seem not to benefit from Primal Therapy are troubled by too much Beta brain wave production and/or insufficient ability to induce an increase in Alpha brain wave production when it is needed.

In Primal Therapy the client lies face up on the floor and repeatedly calls aloud for mommy. Eventually the strangeness of that activity becomes routine—Beta waves diminish—and the monotonous repetition begins to generate the production of Alpha brain waves. There may be other psychological processes going on later in Primal Therapy that I am not aware of. Certainly it is one of the more powerful therapeutic interventions available in the world today.

Biofeedback is very much about generating increased Alpha brain waves. It did not fulfill its promise as a therapeutic intervention because it never occurred to therapists to have clients first create a mental picture of a fear trigger at the heart of what was troubling them. Had the clients then followed up contiguously with the Biofeedback instrument, chances are the simple, hand-held Biofeedback instrument would have worked as well as AT-T or EMDR. Had it occurred to psychotherapists to do it this way, I suspect Biofeedback instruments would be the premier therapy today and there would be an instrument in almost every household.

Eastern and Middle Eastern cultures offer well developed and sophisticated—and replicable!—techniques involving the induction of altered states of consciousness. Generically known as meditation, we now understand these altered states as induced Alpha and sometimes even Theta brain wave dominance. Western research has demonstrated that daily meditation can be instrumental in developing healthy self-improvement, with no downside risk at all. Most Western behavioral scientists still distrust altered states of consciousness, whereas Eastern scientists and practitioners encourage them in organized, goal-directed systems that offer predictable benefits.

Transcendental Meditation (TM), brought to America by an East Indian Guru—guru simply means teacher in Hindi—known as Maharishi Mahesh Yogi, is a typical case in point. TM has been examined by Western science and has been validated as promoting improved mental, emotional and physical health when practiced briefly on a daily basis. This is significant because it exemplifies how a strange, seemingly unexplainable and—still!—mistrusted practice has been demystified and added to our baseline of scientific knowledge. Having been explained and defined, tested and replicated it can now be considered a part of science.

The role of the psychotherapist will be undergoing a change. An individual might briefly consult an AT-T therapist, but if they develop some skill in identifying their fear triggers and the self-application of the Targeting intervention, they might never again need such professional help. To a considerable extent many individuals can become their own psychotherapist. To such individuals the function of the Fight-or-Flight emotions, anger and fear, will no longer be considered healthy. They will be able to eliminate the triggering of emotions they no longer need and which they have come to recognize as counterproductive.

The Key Role of Alpha Brain Waves

If you close your eyes and mentally picture what it was—or is, or could be in the future—that specifically threatens to trigger some of your fear feelings, virtually any *contiguous* intervention that induces a slight increase of Alpha brain waves for 10 to 20 seconds will likely have the effect of *permanently* reducing or *permanently* eliminating your Fight-or-Flight emotional response to that trigger!

Targeting is a deceptively simple therapeutic intervention. A "Target" is simply the mental picture of an event—better yet, the specific detail of an event—that did trigger, or could trigger, one or more of your fear feelings. A fear trigger can be someone or something in the future you wish to avoid; it can be the memory of someone or something that still haunts you emotionally; it can be something that could not possibly happen, but you fear it anyway! The goal of AT-T is for your nervous system to no longer remember, experience or anticipate that someone or that something as a fear trigger. The change apparently occurs on a neurological level, because it is a permanent change.

The key role is played by the timely induction of Alpha brain waves. In cases where the strategic induction of Alpha brain waves is inhibited by a brain disorder, an unrecognized closed head injury, or one of the several types of attention deficit disorder, it might be necessary for you to practice inducing Alpha brain waves with a hand-held Biofeedback instrument. In other words, you can retrain your brain by creating new brain wave pathways.

The hand-held Biofeedback instrument provides sound feedback and, if desired, a dial that measures your degree of calmness and relaxation. The sound feedback decreases as Alpha brain waves increase. The sound becomes louder as they decrease and Beta waves increase. Increased Alpha brain waves are associated with calmness and relaxation, according to research, and associated reduction of the amount of perspiration released from the pores of the fingers. The hand-held Biofeedback instrument is a reliable device that enables you to build new brain pathways for the conduction of Alpha brain waves. Fortunately, the human brain has remarkable redundancy qualities. You will also learn what it feels like to be calm and relaxed, important qualities for improved problem solving, for sustaining attention and for the highest quality of performance in any activity in which you are engaged at the moment.

All of your brain waves work interactively all the time. In order to pay attention you produce increased Beta waves, but you don't stop producing Alpha waves. In order to think creatively or globally you produce more Alpha waves, but you don't stop producing Beta waves. On the other hand, if you are producing too many Beta waves you are easily distracted. If you are not producing enough Beta waves your mind will tend to wander.

If you are attempting creative writing or creative art, but you are producing insufficient Alpha waves, you just can't seem to get started. If you are producing too many Alpha waves, you tend to keep thinking of ideas that are too abstract or too large, and you keep changing your mind. Put perhaps too simply, you need Alpha brain waves to come up with a creative idea or an overall plan, but you also need Beta brain waves to start it, to keep it organized, and to complete it in a timely manner.

It sounds complicated, doesn't it? In fact, brain wave interaction is extremely complicated. But studies in brain mapping and brain wave training have been in progress for the past several decades and there is already a considerable baseline of knowledge. Put simply, you could think of your brain waves as interacting in a kind of symphony, interacting constantly with each other as you go about your day.

It is known that Beta brain waves play a major role in enabling a person to be consciously aware of information obtained through the physical senses. Humans rely mostly on visual and oral information, provided they are neither blind nor deaf. Humans (and some animals, also) who are impaired in one of the senses often learn to rely on the remaining senses, which sometimes become more acute. Even so, they are sensory and they continue to be the function primarily of Beta brain waves.

Six or eight of the 18 Positive Affirmation Phrases listed on the Targeting worksheet are repeated silently, mentally, with eyes closed, about ten times each—explained in detail in a later chapter. In spite of their obvious positive content and providing direction for self-improvement, that is not their primary purpose. More importantly, the monotony of the repetitions, the absence of the stimulation of the sound of your own voice, the lack of visual stimulation because your eyes are closed, soon reduces the amount of Beta brain waves and induces the increased production of Alpha brain waves. This creates the neurological environment that results in the permanent neutralization of the fear trigger being Targeted. Should the same or a similar trigger be experienced a day or a month or years later, you will not experience it as a fear-inducing event. Any anger, whether internal or external, will also be gone.

Targeting is apparently the only method of psychotherapy that recognizes the strategic importance of Alpha brain waves for therapeutic outcome. When other systems of psychotherapy are successful for the long term it is quite likely that Alpha brain waves were passively—accidentally—generated at the optimal moment. Once the strategic importance of brain wave interaction is better understood this explanation will become obvious to all psychotherapists.

What is required is a good Target—mental picture of what triggered, or would trigger, were it to happen, a fear response—and the contiguous induction of an increase of Alpha brain waves. Any method of therapy—any life experience, for that matter!—will produce positive therapeutic movement *if these two elements are present in the correct order*, whether by accident or by design.

The Twelve Steps program is a sophisticated cognitive recovery program that requires the participant to engage in a structured and progressive self-analysis of the damage to self and to others caused by their addiction. The experiencing of guilt, shame, sadness, disappointment, embarrassment, and so on, at being "out of control" and "unable to resist" using the addictive substance, followed contiguously by a quasi-spiritual ritual that induces Alpha brain waves, would be expected to reduce the associated fear feelings and thereby make abstinence a little easier.

But if a Twelve Steps participant is unable to develop the necessary Alpha brain wave environment, they will find it difficult to establish sobriety through such a program. Beta waves will remain dominant and their fears and resentments will remain essentially intact. In addition, there is at least some risk that by increasing their awareness of all the emotional damage they have caused others and themselves, the Twelve Steps program can actually intensify the craving for the emotional escape provided by the addictive substance and for the comforting companionship of fellow addicts.

This is because the true appeal of all addictive substances is that to some degree they temporarily reduce the production of Beta brain waves, resulting in a reduction in feelings of fear and anger. As a result of alcohol or drug induced reduction of Beta brain waves, one experiences a partial inability to have negative thoughts—such as shame, guilt, embarrassment, remorse and sadness—about the damage done to others and to one's self because of their addiction.

Teen Challenge, a Christian oriented recovery program, encourages the addict to admit to their addicted condition—guilt, shame, etc.—to admit to their craving—nervousness, anxiety, shame, etc.—and then to engage repeatedly in prayer. If this induces a decrease in Beta waves and an increase in Alpha waves, the participant experiences the neutralization of some of their drug or alcohol related self-esteem fear triggers and social status fear triggers, past, present and future. As a result one can gradually become more self-confident in planning for a drug-free future. Of course, to be successful via Teen Challenge the participant must have, or develop, a belief and trust in a Higher Power. Since there is less emphasis on the analysis of damage caused to others and to one's self, there is likely less risk of increased substance craving by those who have difficulty internalizing the idea of a helpful Higher Power.

The effectiveness of some religious practices is due to strategically induced Alpha brain waves, whether purposely or by accident. Truly religious people thereby become better able to let go of hurt, fear, envy, excessive cravings, addictions, competitiveness, anger, resentment, materialism, and so on. As their automatic fear/anger responses decrease, they would be expected to experience greater use of their functional IQ, especially the "higher intellectual levels" that were interfered with by fear triggers and the associated excessive Beta brain waves and decreased Alpha brain waves. They would be expected to find it becoming easier to understand more complex or abstract spiritual teachings. The obvious conclusion is that humans have the ability to become more spiritual—via humanization—by transcending their reliance on the counterproductive Fight-or-Flight instinct through the use of AT-T.

A Word to the Wise Psychotherapist and to Coaches, Teachers, and Parents

Does AT-T Sound Too Good to Be True?

AT-T IS DECEPTIVELY SIMPLE, AS IS Shapiro's EMDR. Any reasonably intelligent parent with or without a high-school diploma can successfully apply AT-T to themselves and to their own grade school kids. A clinician with a master's degree or a Ph.D. in psychology might feel a little uncomfortable with the fact that any individual lacking formal education in psychology can understand how to use AT-T simply by reading the book, can become able to resolve any of their fear triggers they can identify as well as guide their child in resolving their everyday fears. Fear not, parents are not equipped to guide their children in resolving more complex psychological problems. For these, a psychotherapist is required.

But, if you really are in the business of helping clients overcome some of their emotion based or emotionally reinforced problems, then you should be glad that psychotherapy is easier than you thought in so many cases. Is your goal really to do psychotherapy, or do you really prefer teaching social skills, thinking skills, decision-making skills and problem solving skills?

Maybe you should consider becoming a teacher. These skills are currently not at all well taught in elementary schools, and the need is great.

You are challenged to apply the AT-T intervention to several of your own self-esteem and social status fears. You are in for the surprise of your life! Especially if you're looking for a method of therapy that works virtually 100% of the time. I've written this book so you could know about it; it's in your hands now. Due directly to its simplicity and its apparent superficiality, the first few times you use it on yourself you will seriously question whether your tests of its effectiveness on yourself were valid. Maybe it was a coincidence that your fear of someone or some situation suddenly went away. Try it on something that REALLY SCARES THE HELL OUT OF YOU. *Assign yourself the task of proving that it doesn't work (!), using yourself as the test subject.*

The first five or six times I used it—granted, it was in a much more complicated format devised by Ken Keyes—I quickly rationalized that perhaps my "fear triggers" were not really fear triggers after all. Then I rationalized that perhaps the fear triggers were so transient that they would have simply dissolved on their own, had I just waited a little longer. Almost out of desperation—after all, I had been trained in several cognitive therapy systems, although they didn't work—I reasoned that there must have been some other reason why my fear feelings had become disconnected from some of their triggers. Last, but not least, I assumed for a while that perhaps I was more suggestible than I realized because of the respect in which I held Key Keyes and his staff.

Eventually, though, I had to admit the truth. The methodology, as complicated as it was at that time, truly did do what Ken Keyes and his staff said it would do. Complicated? There were twelve Positive Affirmation Phrases, which participants were required to memorize, word perfect—we were each required to recite them from memory upon our arrival at the training—and also required to recite aloud from memory for each fear trigger. The first one was: "I am freeing myself from security, sensation and power addictions, which make me try to forcefully control situations in my life, and thus keep me from being able to love myself and others." There were eleven more and they became progressively more esoteric and complex.

The psychotherapist or counselor who has not tested AT-T on herself or himself will not have enough confidence in this therapeutic intervention to tackle a client's complex psychological problems unless she or he has personally verified its effectiveness. It will seem far more comfortable to fall back on the familiar—tried and usually failed—cognitive therapies so popular in most treatment programs.

Assuming the prospective AT-T psychotherapist or counselor has done their personal validation of this methodology, and has thereby become confident that it does work, it is time to begin using it with clients. Not knowing what to expect, the new client will have to experience a similar personal validation. The first fear triggers treated with AT-T will usually be some that are less threatening for the client to disclose to the psychotherapist. This is to be expected, and is actually an indication the client has fairly healthy personal boundaries. Even the simplest fear triggers must be clear and specific, since experience has shown that the nervous system cannot disconnect fear feelings from generalities. For instance, "I worry that I'm too dumb to go to a community college." That's a workable fear trigger for AT-T. "I'm afraid of Democrats, or I'm afraid of Republicans" is not a workable fear trigger. It's too general, so it won't work using AT-T.

Another example: Giving a speech or playing an instrumental solo or singing a solo is not a fear trigger. But the possibility of forgetting what to say can be a fear trigger; the possibility of making a mistake in your performance can be a fear trigger; the possibility of someone in the audience falling asleep can be a fear trigger; the possibility of someone in the audience whispering and giggling can be a fear trigger; the possibility of someone in the audience looking bored can be a fear trigger. The mere anticipation that such things could happen, days before the event, can make them fear triggers because you picture what you are worrying about and therefore your nervous system—not your brain—reacts as if it were happening right now. *If you can identify fear triggers in advance, you can use AT-T to permanently disconnect them in advance.* Then, should any of these things—or similar things—actually occur during your performance, they will not be fear triggers! You will not have a fear-type reaction; instead, you will just notice them, if at all, as benign "things that just happen sometimes."

In a beginners group situation you could ask each participant to close their eyes and to imagine the "most horrible way to die." They might come up with some gruesome examples: sharks, burned alive, buried alive, etc. Each one will have a facial expression that reflects to some degree how awful they feel such an experience would be. Instruct them to silently, mentally, repeat ten times an Affirmation Phrase from the menu that you will say aloud. After each participant has silently repeated the Phrase ten times they are to put one hand palm down on their knee or desk. When all have done so, choose another Phrase from the menu and say it aloud. Keeping their eyes closed, they will follow the same procedure with the next Affirmation Phrase you say aloud. Do this with seven or eight Affirmation Phrases.

Then ask them to again picture what they had thought would be a most horrible way to die. Every participant will report that they no longer consider the way of dying they had chosen as being so uniquely horrible after all. In fact, it will no longer make them fidgety or uncomfortable to think about it anymore! You will be able to see the truth of this in their facial expressions. You will have made your point!

A potential AT-T psychotherapist will wonder whether the intervention is applicable to a client who has a thought disorder, or perhaps a valid diagnosis of psychosis. The answer is, I don't know. Sometimes it might work and sometimes it might be incorporated into the client's delusional thinking. I have not yet found any research on the brain wave patterns of people with thought disorders or psychosis. I suspect, though, that there is a dysfunction in Beta/Alpha brain wave interaction. Needless to say, trying AT-T with a psychotic patient should be undertaken in a fairly secure area because it has not been sufficiently tested on clients with more serious disorders. I have not had the opportunity to test AT-T under such circumstances.

Sometimes medication is an aid to AT-T treatment, with non-psychotic depression, for example, or dysthymia. Remember, AT-T is intended to neutralize fear triggers, and it relies on the timely induction of increased Alpha brain waves. A mildly depressed client often has difficulty identifying their fear triggers; to them it might seem life is just bad, and then you die. An antidepressant can enable them to differentiate among their feelings and to identify their various fear triggers. I have worked successfully with such medicated clients quite often.

I cannot emphasize enough the importance that a psychotherapist, a school counselor, a coach, a schoolteacher, music teacher, drama teacher or a parent first personally validate the effectiveness of AT-T on themselves. It is not realistic to expect someone to sit still for it once they realize you have not pre-tested it on your own fear triggers.

Chapter One
The First Premise: The Fear/Anger Connection

THE FIRST PREMISE OF ALPHA THERAPY-TARGETING (AT-T) is about the connection between fear and anger, more commonly known as the Fight-or-Flight (F-or-F) instinct. Human *fear* functions primarily as an early warning system of impending threat to self-esteem and/or to social status. Human *anger* functions primarily as a defense mechanism, and is automatically activated when such a threat is believed to exist. The perceived threat is called a "fear trigger." It can be the memory of a bad experience with someone or something; it can be someone or something that is currently believed to be presenting such a threat; or it can be someone or something that is perceived as possibly becoming a threat in the future, no matter how unlikely.

Ideally the human F-or-F instinct is gradually replaced by knowledge, understanding, patience, tolerance, insight, spiritual values, social and communication skills, problem solving skills, and so on. With increasing humanity the spontaneous reliance on anger or fear is increasingly recognized as clumsy, primitive, ineffective, and usually counterproductive. As reliance on the F-or-F instinct decreases, one becomes increasingly more "human."

It is a rather new idea in psychology that psychotherapists should be assisting their clients in the direction of eliminating the functions of fear and anger. It gives the psychotherapist an even higher purpose than just improving the client's ability to adjust and adapt more satisfyingly to their problems. While therapy does not, and need not, encroach upon the domain of religion, it seems obvious that therapy and religion should complement each other.

The importance of overcoming various aspects of one's animal nature has been recognized for centuries by the world's major religions, though usually poorly understood and sometimes terribly distorted by some theologians. It will become clear to the reader that many religious practices were (and still are) originally intended in large part to diminish reliance on the F-or-F instinct and thereby produce a better person in both character and healthy spirituality. Some of the goals and practices of religions resonate very well with the methods and goals of the more effective systems of therapy.

The Anthropological Analogy

Anthropologists have long recognized about primitive tribes that the more energy required for simple survival the less energy was available to direct toward higher levels of human functioning. Tribes living in environments where meeting basic survival needs was a constant struggle usually did not have well developed art forms or sophisticated religious beliefs and practices. Tribes in more provident environments usually had more highly developed and sophisticated art forms and religious beliefs and practices.

For instance, the Native American tribes in and around the Great Lakes region of North America enjoyed a varied diet of beans, corn, squash, pumpkins, fish, meat from a variety of animals and birds, a wide variety of wild berries and nuts, wild onions, mushrooms and greens. An enemy tribe called some of these tribes "rattlesnakes" (Iroqu), as an insult. The French added to the original word and after some years most of the tribes in the vast great lakes area became known as Iroquois. Their original name was Haudennosaunne, meaning "People of the Longhouse." Several large tribal groups joined together and established one of the world's earliest democracies. Benjamin Franklin was so impressed with the Haudennosaunne Confederacy that he based the Declaration of Independence on the Confederacy's principles (*http://shannonthunderbird.com/tribal_lifestyle.htm*).

The artwork of the North American Great Lakes region tribes was known to be highly developed also, when compared to that of tribes who lived in areas where the climate and topography made daily survival more difficult. Australian Aboriginals, for example, developed little in terms of art forms, and their clothing and tools, if any, were usually undecorated.

In contrast to the North American Great Lakes region, most of Australia is arid. Native tribes of Australia, of which there are more than five hundred, had to hunt for food every day, largely because they did not develop the means for food preservation. The climate and topography required a nomadic life, and their diet consisted of ants, grubs, caterpillars, lizards, frogs, snakes, rats, opossums, kangaroos, emus, eggs and sometimes fish. There was little time for leisure, except for storytelling, which often consisted of stories about the quest for food. They never came close to developing an agricultural community, raising domestic animals, or otherwise producing their own food. While a few Australian Aborigines have blended into modern society, thousands of them still live the old, primitive lifestyle (*http://www.astronomy.pomona.edu/archo/australia/australia 2.html*).

This anthropological observation is an apt analogy because the same principle applies to individuals who constantly scan for, and protect themselves from, real or imagined threats to their self-esteem and/or social status. Higher mental functions are the first casualties of emotional stress. It is not surprising that individuals who are so constantly on guard for such threats engage in a lot of thinking errors. When the stress is chronic the impairment of higher mental functions tends to be chronic.

Resistance to Giving up Anger and Fear

There is some resistance to the idea of doing away with the F-or-F emotions. This is primarily due to a cultural belief among the educated and the uneducated alike that anger and fear are what give life its vibrancy, and that without them life would be dull and drab. This belief is still prevalent in spite of the fact that the core beliefs of major religions throughout the world—such as Judaism, Islam, Christianity, Hinduism, Buddhism, and many others—have always taught that it is love, appreciation, wisdom, deeper spiritual understanding, patience and compassion that give the greatest satisfaction and vibrancy to one's life, and that it is fear and anger that interferes with one's ability to experience the fullness of these qualities. The fact is, to the extent that one misunderstands the goal of becoming more human and is instead caught up in the anticipation of threats to self-esteem and social status, life does seem more difficult, more frustrating and more futile.

Virtually all religions allow one to pursue violence when physically threatened. But the truly spiritual person of whatever religion is expected to consider the circumstances and to moderate conscientiously the extent of violence that is truly necessary to effectively neutralize a true physical threat. Just as we should not judge Islam by the actions and claims of terrorists, or Buddhism by the self-immolation or violence of protesting monks, we should not judge Christianity or Judaism or Hinduism by some of their extremist or misguided members. The ability to be reasonable in difficult situations is not possible when one's decision to use force is contaminated with fear and anger. This is obviously not primarily a religious issue. It is a problem that troubles all governments, all corporations, all institutions, all races, all cultures, clans and tribes, and even all families.

Another major reason for resistance to the idea of ridding oneself of fear and anger is the belief that it is impossible to do so. Fear and anger are inborn, natural, instinctive and universal. They are supposed to be there! So, over the centuries even educated people have incorporated the natural and seemingly unavoidable functions of fear and anger into their understanding and description of what makes up a healthy human being. Anyone who did not display anger and/or fear occasionally was considered either a saint or a simpleton, and historically neither was to be taken seriously in the real world!

Oddly, the introduction of psychology and the study of human emotions has done little to alter basic cultural beliefs and abuses. Rages, smoldering resentments and acts of revenge are still considered by most people to be somehow self-justifying. Anger is intended to intimidate, and it usually does. While the public display of fear is looked down upon, intimidation to induce fear-based compliance is still used as a control technique in military training and in corporate management. Most therapists still tend to believe that a "reasonable" amount of fear and anger, triggered by "reasonable" causes is a necessary and required part of being a healthy person. *The ridiculous assumption that a certain amount of fear and anger is normal and healthy unavoidably supports the corollary that a certain degree of reduced functional intelligence is therefore normal and healthy, especially in a crisis or emergency—a "reasonable" trigger!*

It is paradoxical that so many people recognize it as obvious that fear and anger interfere with clear thinking, yet educated people in all walks of life still insist that fear and anger are desirable in "reasonable" amounts in "some" situations. We are all culturally conditioned to engage in this circular thinking without question. We only look down our noses at the fear and anger of other people. Most people innocently consider their own fear and anger reasonable and justifiable responses to what they believe to be sufficient causes. Eventually, some people observe that other people's fear and anger episodes are often unreasonable and unjustified. They often find themselves not feeling sympathetic or respectful towards other people's fear or anger. This sometimes starts the mental wheels turning and some individuals begin to insightfully question the legitimacy of their own fear and anger. But such spontaneous insights are rarely lasting. Most people continue to respond to their usual fear triggers with the same fear and/or anger emotions and the same blaming and criticizing, regardless of how ineffective it is and regardless of how often it just makes things worse.

It can be observed that fear and anger are conspicuously absent whenever someone is performing at a level of excellence, whether in sports, entertainment, or public speaking. People perform more skillfully when they forget about the audience and unselfconsciously—fear-lessly—focus on just doing it right, whatever it is. Musicians play best when they are not worrying about mistakes or about music critics, and focus only on the music at hand. The best public speakers and entertainers are those who are not troubled by stage fright or odd behavior by members of the audience. Fear is the physiological energy that prepares a person to run away, so naturally it interferes with any activity where running away is not an option. Anger, which energizes a person to fight, is likewise an unwelcome interference because fighting, whether physically or verbally, seldom is the most viable option.

THE ONE EXCEPTION: There is one type of situation where anger might be considered an asset. When a person's performance is so severely degraded because of intense fear, perhaps to the point of being immobilized, anger can have the effect of temporarily overriding the fear and enabling the person to take at least some form of useful action. A person should not expect this anger-rescue experience to be there when needed, though, because such occurrences are spontaneous and actually rather rare. Obviously this is not a reason to value anger, but it helps to make the case for getting rid of fear. Perhaps this is the origin of the myth that anger resolves fear and improves a person's ability to be assertive.

Some early Vikings admired something called Berserk's Way—

usual English translation—which is described historically as the onset of rage during combat. This was a time and place in history in which wars were fought by brute force with clubs, swords, spears, etc. The Viking warrior could not become "berserk" during combat whenever he wanted to, of course. Sometimes it just happened, unexpectedly. If and when a Viking warrior did become "berserk" during combat, he temporarily had a high pain threshold, was single-mindedly focused on killing or maiming the enemy, and did not tire as quickly as his fellow warriors. It was considered a rageful state of consciousness back then, but it seems analogous to anyone's improved performance when it is without fear. Perhaps it was a cultural expectation that Berserk's Way could only occur during combat. If so, then perhaps the fact that the Berserk Viking warrior was performing unselfconsciously —without fear—was not recognized as the real cause for his becoming such a fearsome and effective fighter. With these rare exceptions, though, it simply isn't true that anger—if that's what "Berserk's Way" really was—improves performance.

Most everyone has observed that during discussion, debate or argument, even a little fear or anger impairs one's ability to be eloquent and verbally persuasive. The stronger the fear or anger the more it causes the deterioration of a person's communication skills. Fearful or angry people cannot easily be reasoned with because strong emotions interfere with higher functional intelligence. It is very difficult to make a serious case for the value of fear or anger as resources for problem solving or otherwise getting one's needs met.

Fear and anger interfere with a person's ability to use whatever insight and experience they possess to choose the most promising approach to problem solving. In spite of the usual variety of options, these emotions always limit a person's ability to make good choices. Fear and anger also interfere with a person's ability to assess whether their immediate strategy is achieving the desired results, or whether it should be intensified, softened or even replaced by an entirely different strategy.

To most people it eventually becomes clear that their anger

and fear are almost always counterproductive. Until recently, though, there has not been very much they could do about it. Individuals burdened with chronic or excessive fear and/or anger were pretty much stuck with it. Cognitive therapies address fear and anger emotions intellectually, and therefore they have not been very effective with the more serious cases. With the introduction of Alpha Therapy, and if there develops a wider application of the EMDR developed by Francine Shapiro, that should begin to change.

The exceptions will likely be those individuals whose fear or anger are neurologically based, or, those who are so frightened by their fear triggers that they refuse therapy and remain in denial. Whenever possible, medication management should be consideration to mitigate against the fear and/or anger problems that are neurologically based. Yet, even in neurological cases, AT-T would enable the client to disconnect some of their fear triggers and perhaps thereby reduce the degree of their dependency on medication.

Chapter Two
The Second Premise: Early Childhood Conditioning

IMPRINTED VALUES—PARADIGMS—ARE TO SOME degree always an obstacle to any individual's growth and development. Paradigms can be defined as "imprinted beliefs and expectations about one's self and imprinted beliefs and expectations about how things and/or other people ought to be." Paradigms are inherently negative by definition—as I define the term—because they are imprinted and therefore resistant to learning and change. Human life, as an experience in learning, growing and changing, is in direct opposition to paradigms. Especially during the first five years of life, a child is almost totally open to being imprinted, but is not yet neurologically developed enough to understand the context.

Paradigms are sanctioned by fear and anger; that is their nature. They work like this: 1. Someone or something causes the individual to feel uneasy, the early warning fear feeling that signal a potential threat to a paradigm; i.e., a fear trigger has been encountered; 2. The individual believes someone or something is threatening, or might threaten, their self-esteem and/or their social status; 3. The individual feeling state changes from uneasy to angry—from fear to anger; from Flight to Fight. This sequence of threat-fear-anger can happen so quickly that the individual is very often unaware that the fear stage even existed!

NOTE: The Alpha Therapy definition of paradigm is not intended to be synonymous with the Jungian concept of archetypes supposedly passed from generation to generation. Yet, it's arguable that racial archetypes are in fact sustained through many generations via imprinting (paradigms), particularly when one considers a child's extreme vulnerability to imprinting during the first five years of life.

It has long been recognized that early childhood experiences —sometimes called conditioning, learning or imprinting—play a key role in the development of values, beliefs, tolerances, character, aspirations, self-esteem and social status. But no one seems to know how to go about managing and socializing children without doing at least some damage to their self-esteem and/or sense of social status. Clinicians who understand the inherent negativity of imprinted paradigms have no idea how to advise parents to rear their children with what might be called "flexible" paradigms, because it is the nature of paradigms to be inflexible. Neither do I. It is fortunate, though, that there is now a way to disconnect the fear triggers that result from the early imprinting of paradigms.

During the first decade of life, children acquire an astonishing amount of information about themselves, about their environment, and about other people, a great deal of which is apparently in the form of paradigms. Some of these imprinted beliefs and expectations are diametrically opposed to each other, while others are terribly distorted or simply not true. The child pays little or no attention to such inconsistency or inaccuracies, and is in fact quite tolerant of such ambiguity of values. In later life, which belief or expectation attains ascendancy over the other is largely dependent upon the mood or emotional state of the individual at the time. As these strange, contradictory values and expectations continue to operate into adulthood, they exist in the individual as a psychological atmosphere of narrow-mindedness and denial. That is, the adult avoids, partly unconsciously, looking at the inconsistencies in many of their beliefs and values.

During their first decade a child is neurologically unable to analyze information, recognize context, compare to previously learned information, or reject anything as untrue. This incredible ability to learn questionable and contradictory values is almost completely a function of imprinting—the spontaneous and automatic establishing of new neural pathways; i.e., paradigms. During the first decade children function as if they considered their parents infallible. They believe their parents are simply behaving the way parents normally behave. Even blatant abuse, however frightening, tends to be perceived by the child as simply what parents do. The child might fear or resent a parent, but will be neurologically unable to recognize a parent's abusive behavior as abnormal.

The child adopts the values—even the contradictory ones—of family elders as they are witnessed from the child's perspective. They have little or no understanding of the context or cause-and-effect of what is happening around them or to them. If a normally non-traumatic experience was perceived by the child as traumatic, then the imprint of that experience will be traumatic and will generate fear triggers. On the other hand, a psychotherapist might recognize a reported childhood experience as inherently traumatic, but if it was not actually perceived that way by the child, the memory of that experience will be found empty of clinically significant fear or anger.

Sometimes a single parent will talk bitterly in front of the child about the uncaring ex-spouse who abandoned them and about how hurtful this was for the child. This can burden the child with artificial hurt and resentment against the missing parent, when in fact the child's bond with, and memory of, that parent might be minimal or even nonexistent. In some traditional therapies the processing of such "informational" issues can waste a lot of therapy time. The quick and effective processing available via

AT-T readily identifies whether these are clinically significant issues, or just a reflection of the parent's resentment.

For Targeting to be successful it is not necessary—and usually not even possible—for the client to remember early traumatic events with any degree of accuracy. Instead, they have become part of the client's general, often distorted, perception of "how life is," or, "how things are," or "how some people are." Individuals are usually unaware of the degree to which they were imprinted during early childhood with self-limiting beliefs and unrealistic expectations. Generally, whoever or whatever triggers an individual's fear and/or anger feelings is considered by that individual to be the cause, and therefore is also considered to be responsible for any ensuing acting out in response. Blaming is learned at an early age by observing one's elders.

Child Abuse Memories

After a number of successful Targeting sessions it is common for a client to begin experiencing a fallout of previously forgotten memories, some accurate and some not so accurate. The Alpha psychotherapist will not hesitate to ask leading questions in order to identify possible fear triggers. Should this elicit a false abuse or trauma memory, it is simply Targeted in the usual way. The immediate outcome of the intervention will make it clear to both therapist and client if it was a false issue, because neither will observe any change in feelings, body language or verbal patterns, and the client will have experienced the performance of the intervention as having been dry and superficial.

Child abuse, especially sexual abuse, can be a touchy area with many therapists. Child abuse seems to call out for retribution or at least confrontation of the alleged perpetrator. However the purpose of AT-T is the elimination, or at least the significant diminishment, of persisting self-esteem and social status problems related to the abuse, and this is accomplished via the AT-T therapeutic intervention, not by confrontation or retribution. The fact is, a client will not experience a sense of "closure" or otherwise benefit emotionally by confronting or punishing the perpetrator.

This of course does not rule out the seeking of consequences and/or psychological treatment for the perpetrator when it is the right thing to do. Certainly if it is suspected the perpetrator might abuse someone else, appropriate action must be taken on behalf of others who might have been sexually abused, or might yet become sexual abuse victims of the perpetrator. The point is, Alpha Therapy as a treatment modality has nothing to do with any actions taken regarding the perpetrator. It is strictly focused on resolution of the client's fear triggers, thereby diminishing related self-limiting or self-defeating thought processes and/or behaviors. Any overt action, legal or otherwise, taken regarding the perpetrator is a practical or ethical decision and should not be construed as part of the client's treatment.

The average individual is not consciously aware of being burdened with self-limiting negative paradigms. They are only aware they cannot tolerate certain situations, certain information or ideas, certain people, certain experiences and certain otherwise reasonable self-esteem or social status risks. Feeling fearful or angry are perceived as "proof" by most individuals that whoever or whatever triggered them is responsible for having caused them. The individual is unaware of the circularity of such reasoning because the fear and anger emotions tend to override rational thinking. The individual's observations that other people are not particularly bothered by similarly intolerable people, situations or ideas is of little help. The client assumes such people are simply too insensitive to appreciate the dilemma. For a person to think otherwise would mean that person is questioning—threatening!— his or her own paradigms.

Negative paradigms make the preservation of one's precarious sense of self-esteem and social status an ongoing, but poorly understood and never resolved, struggle. Virtually everyone suffers to some degree the self-limiting and self-defeating effects of chronic doubts about their self-worth. In a kind of desperation they look to peers for estimates of their day-to-day worthiness. Most people expend more energy than they realize in the ongoing effort to prevent other people from noticing how much in doubt they are about their own personal value. They have accepted it as just a matter of their bad luck in a not very fair world and they usually cannot imagine ever overcoming it. Their adjustment to low self-esteem is to try not to be consciously aware of it and to behave in ways intended to prevent other people from noticing it. Most people distract themselves by engaging in denial and by focusing their attention on the real or imagined faults and shortcomings of other people.

After AT-T progresses—whether guided by a psychotherapist or self-administered—the individual begins to recognize a different sort of reality. *They begin to understand that when they experience anger-based thinking or start acting out anger it is another opportunity to eliminate a fear trigger they didn't know was there.* Real humanization begins to occur when they learn to "catch themselves in the act" of anger-based thinking. Such understanding gives the AT-T client another life-changing opportunity. They can analyze the scenario and mentally picture what was to them the key fear stimulus and then perform the AT-T therapeutic intervention on themselves. Or, they can make a note to tell their Alpha psychotherapist about it at the next therapy session and thereby receive guidance in applying the intervention.

The point is that it can take awhile for an individual to become aware of the negativity of their paradigms. It is rarely obvious to an individual that paradigms, and their "offspring," fear triggers, are the primary self-limiting and self-defeating factors in their life. It is the triggering of any of the forms of fear or anger that the AT-T client begins to recognize as evidence of the existence of a threat to a paradigm.

The terms subconscious, unconscious, preconscious, etc., refer to whatever is neurologically recorded as memory, but is not currently recalled into that person's conscious awareness. It is well established that original negative imprinting need not be consciously remembered in order to guide a person's perceptions, interpretations and emotional responses. The AT-T psychotherapist does not need to venture aggressively into what is not readily recalled by the client. Whether the mental picture is of a feared event that has not yet happened, a feared event that probably could never happen, or a feared event that can be only symbolically pictured mentally—such as an imagined flaw that precludes success or lasting happiness—it is a fear trigger, a Target, and it can be neutralized via the AT-T intervention.

Imagine that a particular un-recalled childhood trauma has produced certain fear triggers. This is the equivalent of an inflexible paradigm. This paradigm can be threatened in a variety of ways, each of which triggers some form of the original fear, and possibly a subsequent activation of the anger defense mechanism. If the client Targets each fear trigger at the first opportunity after it is experienced and identified as such, the associated negative imprint—paradigm—is gradually weakened, even though it might never be consciously remembered by the client. With sufficient reduction of the fear triggers it generated, the fact that the original trauma remains un-recalled is unimportant.

Philosophically, Alpha Therapy is considered incomplete until the individual's fear and/or anger emotions no longer significantly interfere with the individual's ability to think rationally and to interact with reality as it is, instead of how he or she wishes it were. Although rather idealistic—and seemingly unattainable—the treatment is theoretically incomplete until the F-or-F instinct is rendered completely dormant. But when an individual displays a relatively calm and assertive, but non-blaming, recognition of the general origin of their fears and anger, combined with acceptance of total personal accountability for obtaining resolution of all the fear triggers they encounter, they are on their way to true humanity.

It requires some courage to seek psychotherapy. Yet, an individual does so with the hope that the therapist will view their presenting problems in approximately the same way they themselves do. In other words, they take their various paradigms right into therapy with them. Sometimes the Alpha psychotherapist is "ambushed" by an unexpected fear trigger or by a fear trigger in an unexpected scenario. A client who is normally untroubled by an associate might be extremely intolerant of them under certain circumstances; a client who is normally compassionate towards gays and lesbians might be extremely homophobic under certain circumstances. The therapist might be surprised when a client is offended by what was considered a casual, harmless or even helpful comment.

A client might suddenly become noncompliant because one day the therapist reminds him or her of a relative who was abusive during the client's early childhood. The client might be unaware of the reason for their sudden dislike or distrust of the therapist. Upon noticing the change in the client's affect and their sudden tendency to be noncompliant, the Alpha psychotherapist can assist the client in analyzing their immediate thoughts and/or memories. It's a good idea anyway to periodically direct a client to Target the AT-T psychotherapist her—or himself. From time to time the AT-T psychotherapist does in fact become a fear trigger because she or he is encouraging the client to become consciously aware of a new area of fear triggers.

Chapter Three
The Third Premise: Anger Is a Defense Mechanism

ANGER IS A DEFENSE MECHANISM. IT is triggered by threats to one's sense of social status and/or self-esteem. In other words, it is activated by fear triggers. This is the most difficult premise for many individuals, especially males, to accept. The anger response is always secondary to a fear response. This means that some form of fear, including anticipatory fear, precedes anger, if only for an infinitesimal moment. This includes anger that is only expressed internally, by mentally criticizing someone or something when there is no practical reason for doing so. The greater the perceived threat—even if it is imaginary—the stronger the anger response can be. *Fear* in any of its forms—worry, anxiety, nervousness, embarrassment, disappointment, jealousy, guilt, shame, hurt, sadness, etc.—creates the sensation of being weak, vulnerable, alone and not in control. *Anger* in any of its intensities—irritation, hostility, disdain, frustration, annoyance, impatience, rage, hate, indignation, resentment, etc.—creates the illusion of being right, empowered, independent, focused, and so on.

NOTE: Before going on to explain this principle, a significant variation should be pointed out. Occasionally the Alpha psychotherapist encounters a client who as a child observed an adult use anger to elicit obedience or compliance. In such circumstances the child learns to "produce anger" for the same purposes. If the child's imitative anger elicits approval and occasionally some degree of compliance it eventually becomes automatic behavior. It is analogous to giving orders in an unnecessarily loud voice. It is not true anger, and it is not being used as a defense mechanism. Once self-esteem fears and social status fears in other areas have been neutralized, however, the client can become aware of their inappropriate use of "anger" and choose to change that behavior.

Most of society and most therapists still perceive anger as a separate, free-standing emotion, only occasionally related to fear. Because the capacity to feel fear and anger exists, most people assume they have a healthy purpose. Many educated people believe anger enables an individual to be more assertive. For example, a woman who suffers an abusive husband is usually encouraged by abuse shelter staff to feel more anger. While anger occasionally—though rarely—does enable a person to overcome numbing fear and to take at least some action, any psychotherapist or counselor who encourages a client to become more angry apparently doesn't know what else to do.

Yet, wouldn't one expect a psychotherapist or counselor to be aware that anger interferes with rational thought? The abused woman can be influenced at an abuse shelter to learn that anger does indeed feel better than fear. As she generates increased anger she receives the approval of abuse shelter staff. But the woman must continue to feel the anger in order to sustain the momentum of her anger-based assertiveness. Unfortunately, her anger is there in sufficient strength only as long as she feels the support and encouragement of the abuse center staff. This is because her underlying fear will continue to undermine her self-confidence.

The Alpha Therapist's approach would be to guide her in

Targeting her self-esteem fear triggers, as well as fear triggers directly related to the abusive husband or boyfriend. These would include fear threats that have occurred and could occur again, fear threats that have not actually occurred but might, and those that are highly improbable or even imaginary. The latter two are anticipatory fear triggers, yet the fears they cause are just as real. The use of AT-T would significantly and permanently diminish her fear of the abusive husband and thereby enable her to make the necessary decisions for her own well-being. More importantly, she would be able to follow through on those decisions without being emotionally dependent on the support and approval of the abuse shelter staff.

Observations of animals clearly demonstrates the limitations and risks inherent in reliance on fear and anger emotions. Wolf packs frighten deer into running until the weaker or younger deer fall behind. When animals are enraged or afraid they usually behave in an exaggerated fashion. Even pets can become emotionally unstable and even dangerous when their fear and anger are triggered. Human beings are not very different from animals when their self-esteem or social status is threatened by fear triggers.

The anger defense mechanism is sometimes not activated at all and the individual experiences fear feelings without becoming angry. All anger is preceded by fear. Frequently it is anticipatory fear. But fear does not always activate the anger defense mechanism. Most of the time the anger defense mechanism is not externally observable, likely due to early childhood imprinted paradigms that disallow expressions of anger under certain circumstances. It is more commonly expressed in demeaning or devaluing thoughts and judgments about the person or situation that represents the fear trigger, and is shared only with others the individual assumes will agree with their demeaning judgments.

Early childhood experiences imprint the child with paradigms that require them to maintain the fear in some situations as a means of avoiding responsibility and/or getting dependency needs met. Some paradigm imprints dictate that the child must remain fearful and should not become angry—at least outwardly! The existence of fear triggers that activate the anger defense mechanism are also the result of early childhood paradigm imprints.

Individuals who have fairly severe anger or rage problems often cannot entertain the possibility that their anger is fear induced, even though they realize their anger is usually counterproductive or at least inappropriate. Even though many rageful individuals are aware of having an anger problem and are in fact troubled by it, yet they usually continue to blame it on the person or the situation that seemingly caused it. If the therapist directs the client to use the Affirmation Phrase, "I don't have to be angry," this can temporarily—at least during the therapy session—reduce their degree of dependency on anger. This kind of anger reduction is only temporary, a "halo" effect, because the unrealized fear still exists. But this sometimes enables the rageful individual to at least consider the possibility that their anger might be fear based.

Anger, in a sense, rescues the individual from having to endure the extremely unpleasant emotions associated with feeling like a victim. Who would want to give up the sense of power, even if it is anger-based, and usually counterproductive, when their imprinted value is that the only alternative is to live with fear and to feel powerless and socially isolated? Hence the difficulty in obtaining the cooperation of a client who has a rage problem.

It is a serious mistake for a psychotherapist to not recognize anger as a defense mechanism. Since the client is usually totally unaware that fear is the root cause of his or her anger, it can be like the blind leading the blind! Each time the Alpha psychotherapist guides a client in Targeting a fear trigger the client comes closer to a realization that anger is a secondary emotion. But since everyone has a variety of fear trigger scenarios, when a newer client has another rage incident, he or she will once again be blind to the fact that it was the result of an unrecognized fear trigger. Once again the anger defense mechanism hides the fear from the experiencer. When the anger scenario is analyzed in the next therapy session and the fear elements identified, the client will be amazed they failed to recognize it when it happened.

Chapter Four

SELF-ESTEEM IS INNATE. WHAT INTERFERES WITH one's self-esteem are paradigms that are learned—imprinted—during early childhood. With the possible exception of brain damage, self-esteem cannot be destroyed. Paradigms imprinted in early childhood produce inflexible values, beliefs and expectations about one's self, about one's world and about the people in it. Anyone or anything that challenges—threatens—one's paradigms is reacted to as a fear trigger. Due to imprinted paradigms many situations and people in an individual's life are perceived as fear triggers. Since life challenges us to grow, to develop and to change, almost on a daily basis every individual experiences the "immovable object meeting the irresistible force!" One's sense of self-esteem and sense of social status are the unavoidable casualties. As Alpha Therapy-Targeting (AT-T) successfully neutralizes fear triggers, the paradigms that caused them are weakened and innate self-esteem is gradually liberated.

As already explained in Chapter Two, paradigms are imprinted beliefs or expectations about how things and/or how people ought to be, and beliefs and expectations about how oneself is, or ought to be. All imprinted paradigms are negative due to their inflexibility and because they are reinforced by fear and often anger. The seemingly "locked in" values of imprinted paradigms are usually learned during the first decade of life.

It is unfortunate that positive values such as self-worth, honesty, integrity, fairness to others, altruism, a sense of community, work ethic, healthy curiosity, appreciation of spiritual pursuits, an optimistic outlook, respect for parents, and so on, are usually imprinted as inflexible paradigms. They seem like good values, except that no values, even good ones, should be set in emotional cement! Have you ever heard of an inflexible paradigm that dictated the individual must be flexible, must learn, and by learning must grow and change? Neither have I! But I wish I knew how to instruct parents to instill such paradigms in their children.

There are no perfect parents and no perfect families. There is a saying that "all families are dysfunctional, but some are more dysfunctional than others," and this is fundamentally true. This is not to say that every individual needs a therapist. But even the emotionally and mentally healthiest people have had to overcome some of the negative effects of their imprinted paradigms. Many adults haven't had much success in this regard, and live in frustration because the learning experiences in their lives are so often at odds with their imprinted values and expectations.

The fact that self-esteem is inborn and only interrupted by learned negative paradigms is evidenced by the outcome of successful psychotherapy. It can be seen in improvements in such things as insight, adaptability, posture, gait, voice modulation, assertiveness, self-confidence, and so on, depending upon which of these qualities were being interfered with by the fear triggers that were neutralized via AT-T. It is presumptuous to assume that self-esteem is "recreated" through successful psychotherapy. It makes more sense to observe that self-esteem reappeared because it was always there, held in check by the fear triggers generated by negative or unfulfillable paradigms. As obvious as this might seem, it has never been clearly defined or outspokenly accepted by anyone, including psychotherapists.

Certain life experience, such as a near-death experiences, or marriage and child birth can produce a therapeutic or otherwise enlightening effect. Yet such experiences usually fail to do so. Paradigms seem to compartmentalize one's thinking. Many individuals have a remarkable ability to resist integrating new information or perceptions with information already imprinted. They either can not or will not consider altering a preconceived belief or point of view, and as a rule, they usually consider their rigidity a sign of their good character.

Higher education is often assumed to have a humanizing effect that instills and/or validates all the best human qualities in an individual. But higher education is commonly compartmentalized, unconsciously, so as not to disturb imprinted, inflexible paradigms. It is sometimes even selectively distorted by students so as to reinforce negative beliefs and expectations. Paradigms are reinforced by fear and anger, whereas new knowledge usually is not. That is why new knowledge is frequently distorted or misunderstood so as to preserve paradigms. Information that does not threaten one's paradigms, even rather obviously inaccurate information, is often welcomed and integrated into one's personal fund of "knowledge."

What happens when a key paradigm is threatened? Consider the movement toward ordination of female priests and female rabbis. Consider modern research that throws doubt on the historical accuracy of the Old Testament. What if God is more like an extraterrestrial than a human or "spirit?" Consider the male employee whose female supervisor or co-worker is obviously smarter and more competent than he is, and she is lesbian and legally married to another woman, and they are adopting a child? New ideas of the preceding kinds are rejected out of hand by some people, and cause near panic in others. Such ideas are considered interesting and intriguing by some people, even by those who do not readily accept them as appropriate. It clearly depends upon one's paradigms, particularly those paradigms that are the most strongly reinforced by fear and anger.

Parts of Western culture seem burdened with a paradigm that overemphasizes the importance of personal assertiveness and material acquisition. This paradigm usually includes the requirement that a person's assertiveness and material acquisition be of a quality and kind that is visible and can thereby earn other people's approval and admiration. This materialistic paradigm is reinforced by the fear of personal insufficiency, the fear of material insufficiency and the fear of being seen by others as inferior. Generally speaking, the "have nots" feel embarrassed and disappointed and are envious of the "haves," which produces resentment toward wealthier people.

Materialistic and assertiveness paradigms are very real concerns, strongly felt at various times by most people. But excessive assertiveness never resolves an individual's fear of being under-assertive. Excessive material acquisition never generates a sense of material sufficiency. And neither one will alleviate one's fears of being perceived as inferior. A healthy sense of personal and material sufficiency can only be regained if one can neutralize the fear triggers that reinforce such paradigms. As a result, one's assertiveness and work ethic will be more reality oriented and there will remain a reasonable and healthy appreciation of the opinions of others.

The therapeutic Targeting of one's fear triggers is a far better meaning for the term "facing your fears." Terms intended as encouragement, such as "keep a stiff upper lip," "grin and bear it," "hang in there," "just ignore it," "don't pay any attention to that," and so on, will hopefully some day fall into disuse. No matter how well meant such advice, or how warmly offered, they discourage resolution of the problem and are more likely to result in the chronic harboring of resentment. *It is important to point out that a fear trigger continues to undermine one's self-esteem and sense of social status even when one isn't thinking about it.* Although seldom consciously realized, resentment does not neutralize a fear trigger;

instead it complicates the problem by interfering with the individual's awareness of the real problem, which is the threat of feeling one or more of the various types of fear.

Chapter Five
The Importance of Mental Imagery

PART OF OUR BRAIN IS AWARE of a past, a present and a future. But the part of our brain that controls our Fight-or-Flight (F-or-F) emotions, anger and fear, reacts as if whatever we are thinking about is happening right now. This is why there are such things as painful memories, worries about the future, happily looking forward to a vacation, and why we don't like to think about some things and why we don't like to have someone remind us of unpleasant memories. We spend most of our waking hours picturing whatever we happen to be thinking about.

A person can worry about an upcoming event well before it happens, or worry about an event that is not even likely to happen. A person sometimes finds it difficult to pay attention to details on the job a few days before a vacation is due to start. Children and adults alike enjoy a story, a movie or an anecdote. As a person listens to someone telling about something, the listener mentally visualizes the events as they unfold, and vicariously experiences them. Talk about slicing a lemon, squeezing lemon juice, or making lemonade for a while and anyone who is listening will begin to salivate. They are visualizing what you are talking about and their nervous system reacts as if what they are visualizing is real and happening right now.

Ask a heterosexual male whether he would prefer, if required, to watch a pornographic movie about gay men or one about lesbian women. He will spontaneously create an image in his mind of each possible movie scenario. Unless he is actually gay himself, he will react with disgust at his mental picture of gay men engaging in sex, but will blush at his mental picture of lesbian pornography, which he finds slightly erotic.

Writers of novels and movies have only a limited array of story lines to portray if they hope to sell a lot of books or tickets or videos. If they wander too far from people's expectations or go so far as to threaten their paradigms, their novels or movies will not be considered entertaining by very many people, the educated and the uneducated alike, and they will not sell at all well.

This is an important fact of human psychology because so many people live their lives either partly or largely according to what they mentally visualize. Part of the time all people live their lives, without realizing it, in a fantasy version of reality. Why they do this is a subject for the combined study by anthropologists, sociologists and psychologists. But there is no question that it's true. Marketers and advertisers have been aware of this fact for a long time and regularly use it in order to sell products, services and entertainment.

Since there are no perfect parents, all parents make mistakes. Some examples are over-punishing, excessive pressuring to succeed in school or in sports, and so on. It is often difficult to tell when child-rearing methods cross the line and become abusive. During the first decade of life children are like little learning machines. A normal, healthy infant or toddler cannot "not learn." This is a time when new neural pathways record and preserve virtually every experience, from the child's perspective of course, with little or no awareness or intent on the child's part. Prime examples are the learning of the family language, the family member's roles, racial biases and religious biases.

In addition to the family language, the child is imprinted with a variety of paradigms regarding *when* and *why* they are worthy and lovable, when and why they are unworthy and unlovable, as well as how they *should* be and how other people and things *should* be. As stated elsewhere in this book, there are no good paradigms. This is because paradigms are naturally inflexible and therefore they put an emotional lock on the person's ability to refine, by learning, growing and changing, what they believe and what they understand.

In human individuals, the F-or-F emotions, anger and fear, are essentially in the service of preserving paradigms. The working efficiency of the brain, especially at its higher levels of functioning, begins to break down whenever the F-or-F emotions are triggered. This is generally referred to as stress, although in reality it means one or more of the individual's paradigms are being threatened. Stress is usually blamed on something external, such as a stressful job, a stressful event, or another person, such as a demanding boss, someone criticizing, someone making a rude comment, etc. Seldom does a person recognize that stress comes from within and is one's own emotional reaction to a paradigm-generated fear trigger.

True self-esteem, poorly understood by most people, is a person's recognition of their humanness as a midway point between animal and something beyond merely being fully human. True self-esteem enables a person to avoid becoming overly focused on materialism, social climbing, social recognition, competition, power over others, to name just a few. Most religions allude to something worth striving for beyond merely being a competent, successful human being, so the idea that a psychotherapist would entertain such an esoteric concept should not be considered so very odd. What might be considered odd is the therapist who is in denial about there being such a possibility. This is the area where psychotherapy could, and should, resonate with the core spirituality of religions—as opposed to the organizational structure of religions.

Of course, the Alpha therapist's role is simply to assist the client in identifying their fear triggers and to guide them in their neutralization. Put differently, the Alpha therapist assists the client in eliminating as much as possible the interfering effects of their negative paradigms. The more success an individual has neutralizing fear triggers, the more able he or she is to consider the next goal, that of seeking what lies beyond the mere experiencing of a human life. It is not the therapist's role to define what lies beyond being human or to provide guidance in finding out. That is usually thought to be the role of religions, but perhaps intuition becomes the true guide once fear and anger have been largely eliminated.

Society—and many a psychotherapist—has always jumped on the blaming bandwagon. Much more empathy should be felt by therapists for the incredibly difficult task of rearing emotionally healthy children. Psychotherapists should be the least likely to fall into the trap of blaming every client's problems on the parents. Certainly there are toxic—a currently popular term denoting someone who has a strong negative effect on a child's self-esteem—parents, toxic kids, toxic teachers, toxic relatives and even toxic friends. It's sometimes necessary for the therapist to recognize them for the client's sake. But the next step should be to enable the client, via the AT-T therapeutic intervention, to overcome their fears of the toxic aspects of a person and thereby become able to make whatever decisions or take whatever actions are necessary and appropriate.

After acknowledging there are no perfect parents and that they all make mistakes, the Alpha psychotherapist needs to stop blaming them. While it's not the client's fault that she or he has self-esteem problems or social status problems, it is the client's responsibility, in cooperation with a competent therapist—and the responsibility of a competent therapist, in cooperation with a willing client—to identify and to neutralize the fear triggers that play such a major role in the client's life. If a parent is the fear trigger in certain situations, which is common, he or she is Targeted in exactly the same manner as is any other fear trigger.

Imprinting from early childhood has a great effect on the kind of mental imagery in the mind of every adult individual. Unfulfillable or unrealistic beliefs or expectations—the negative paradigms—interfere with functional intelligence, generate mental imagery that is out of sync with reality, and produce mental and emotional disorders—those that are not neurological. Unrealized fear triggers generated by imprinted paradigms cause a person to have maladaptive, judgmental reactions to many people and to many situations. These reactions are characterized by fear, anger, blaming, avoidance, denial, and various other thinking errors. The individual assumes their judgment is reasonably accurate and their blaming valid and justified. Most of their attention remains focused on the unfairness of other people or situations. Unaided by an Alpha psychotherapist, they rarely become aware that their intolerance is fear-based.

An individual's mental imagery can be self-limiting in one situation and self-actualizing in another. A person who is open to self-actualization or enlightenment or self-realization—there are many such esoteric and spiritual terms—is not responding to an imprinted paradigm as the term is used in this book. This is because such esoteric concepts imply significant changes in a person's perception of themselves and their perception of others and of existence in general. For most people, to be open to even considering such significant and basic changes is to challenge many, if not all, of one's imprinted paradigms. Addressing them tends to require considerable courage, even with the help of an AT-T psychotherapist.

Though paradigms tend to be hidden from a person's conscious mind, they are definitely there and they are definitely interfering with self-esteem, with relationships, and with virtually every kind of activity. Anger, in one form or another, is the defense mechanism that protects a person from having to be continually aware of the fear associated with their self-limiting paradigms. There is a saying that "everyone needs someone to look down on." By being critical of others an individual is using the mechanism of blaming—which is anger-based—to avoid having to be continually aware of their own fear triggers and the kinds of fear they invoke. With humans, this seems to be an almost automatic response. But only the ability to feel fear and anger are instinctive; how frequently and how strongly these feelings are activated is not instinctive. It is learned.

As previously mentioned, it is not necessary to identify the actual origin of a paradigm in order to liberate enough of an individual's self-esteem and to restore most of their normal functional intelligence. AT-T addresses the client's current personal reality; that is, their current fear triggers. What they worry about, what they resent, what irritates them, what hurts their feelings, what embarrasses them, what bores them, and so on. These are all symptomatic of fear triggers. The recognition that current self-esteem problems originate in paradigms imprinted in early childhood simply provides a unifying context. That is sufficient. Whatever the actual paradigm, its inflexibility is weakened as the fear triggers it generated are neutralized via the AT-T intervention.

It becomes clear that a person's mood, as well as the state of their self-esteem, is closely related to their mental imagery. This is why it makes so much sense that the focus of AT-T is on the client's mental image of fear triggers. Some individuals will have experienced as traumatic what others will have experienced as benign. The focus of AT-T is always on *reality as experienced by the client*. The recognition of each individual client's fear triggers is what guides the direction of a series of Alpha Therapy sessions, regardless of their similarity or dissimilarity to any other client's fear triggers.

Chapter Six
Identifying Fear Targets

THE GENERIC TERM FOR ALPHA THERAPY is Targeting. One's fear triggers are the "Targets" of Alpha Therapy (AT-T). By fear triggers is meant the people, the things, the situations or the personal flaws—whether real or imagined—that trigger one's feelings of nervousness, embarrassment, hurt feelings, grief, shame, disappointment, anxiety, jealousy, and so on. Anger, whether mild—as in annoyance—or severe—as in rage or hate—is a secondary emotion because it is directed at who or what an individual perceives as the "cause" of their fear and/or anger feelings. Therefore, anger is a defense mechanism: There are no anger triggers as such! Not every fear experience activates the anger defense mechanism, of course. But, put simply, when there is no fear, there is no anger.

An Alpha Therapy Target is one's mental picture of the part of an unpleasant or traumatic experience that made it a fear-inducing experience, and that part is called a fear trigger. It can be something that happened a long time ago, because of which one is still unconsciously carrying the fear and/or resentment; it can be a currently active experience; or, it can be the mental picture of an anticipated fear experience. The part of the brain associated with the Fight-or-Flight emotions, fear and anger, does not differentiate between past, present and future. So mentally picturing a fear trigger, whether old, current, anticipated or highly unlikely, can still generate some of the fear and/or anger as if it were happening right now.

The F-or-F instinct in humans is fundamentally the same as that in animals. As already explained, only the nature of the fear triggers is different. The human F-or-F emotional response became specialized and more complex, possibly due to social conditioning. Real or imagined threats to one's sense of self-esteem or social status are far more often what trigger some form of fear, as well as the anger defense mechanism.

Extreme forms of fear are more readily displayed publicly and more readily admitted to because they are less easily hidden from one's own conscious awareness and from public view. Fear in relatively milder forms, such as worry, nervousness, embarrassment, jealousy, guilt, and hurt are more likely to be hidden from an individual's conscious awareness as well as hidden from public view. Milder intensity of the anger defense mechanism is more commonly expressed internally in angry thinking, dislike, mental criticism, blaming and passive-aggressive forms of revenge.

Circular thinking enables the angry person to believe their anger "proves" they are "right" to devalue and blame whoever or whatever they believe "caused" their anger. As already mentioned, an individual engaging in such circular thinking rarely recognizes it as such. In fact, much of the denial and justification of F-or-F emotional reactions is actually considered socially acceptable. Most people, whether trained in psychology or not, seldom question denials of fear and justifications of anger.

One might imagine a bell curve representing the degrees of denial and justification of F-or-F emotional reactions. On one side of the bell curve is a small percentage of people who exhibit pathological fear and/or pathological anger. The majority in the middle of the bell curve exhibit "socially acceptable" denial of fears and justifications of anger—blaming and criticizing. On the other side of the bell curve is a small percentage of people who have intuited—or just used logic—that fear and anger are primitive, clumsy and counterproductive.

Since it is impossible for a child to exercise enough control over their environment to prevent or avoid self-esteem threats, denial modeled by their elders quickly becomes the most used defense mechanism. Usually the effective use of the anger defense mechanism does not develop until the latter half of the child's first ten years. But even mild threats to self-esteem are like a gentle but persistent push in a self-limiting direction. Being in denial does not prevent self-esteem threats from continually undermining self-esteem and interfering with functional intelligence and performance.

Both client and therapist need to be alert to cues in body language, tone of voice, verbal expression, passive-aggressive attitude and devaluing thoughts commonly associated with fear triggers. If the symptoms are there, the threat to self-esteem is significant. Therapeutic life experiences do occur. They are considered therapeutic if they result in the permanent neutralization of one or more fear triggers, in which case there is no longer evidence of denial, justification or devaluing associated with those fear triggers.

Anger is a defense mechanism, but it can also be considered a form of denial. Anger enables a person to spontaneously relegate fear feelings to near non-awareness. Anger enables a person to become "innocently" unaware that a fear trigger was actually the true cause of their anger. The angry person feels more confident in the face of the fear trigger by indulging confidently in the temporary illusion of being empowered, and "depersonalizes" the problem via criticism, blaming, disdain, irritation, annoyance, indignation, hostility, resentment, and other anger-based devaluing thoughts or actions directed toward the perceived "cause."

As already mentioned, fear generates the sensation of being weak, alone and not in control, whereas anger creates the temporary illusion of being empowered, independent and in control. Anger simply feels better than fear even though it is primarily a band-aid for one's threatened self-esteem or threatened sense of social status.

At worst, the part of the brain associated with fear and anger "believes" the mentally pictured dreaded trip next week to the dentist is happening right now; it "believes" the feared flu shot being pictured is happening right now. *At best*, it "believes" remembered or anticipated pleasant events are happening right now, too. But what is truly *the very best* is that what the person is dreading—mentally picturing—right now presents an opportunity to use the AT-T therapeutic intervention to permanently neutralize it as a fear trigger. The emotional wound, so to speak, is reopened and it represents another opportunity to become more humanized, more intelligent and more self-confident.

Should there be any doubt regarding the validity of a fear trigger, it only takes a few minutes to apply the Targeting intervention. Very little time is "wasted" and the question is cleared up. The worst outcome would be that there would be no outcome, and one moves on in search of real fear triggers. It makes no difference whether the fear feelings are in anticipation of public speaking, an upcoming job interview, auditioning for a part in a play or movie, final exams or SATs in school, preparing to sing or play a solo, or sports competition. All can be quickly eliminated in advance via the AT-T intervention.

The Alpha psychotherapist can empathize or otherwise show compassion for the client's emotional suffering, but the client must begin to understand that their fear and anger originate within themselves. It is understandable that a new client might find this rather difficult to accept at first. But acceptance becomes easier as the client discovers with the guidance of an Alpha psychotherapist, and eventually by self-application of the AT-T intervention, that because they themselves are the immediate originators, their fears and anger can be drastically reduced and perhaps eliminated. It is a unique form of personal ownership and the AT-T therapeutic intervention enables a client to transform it into a unique form of personal empowerment.

In order to identify key fear elements for Targeting the client must resist their misguided seeking of comfort and avoidance of discomfort by constantly scanning for threats to their sense of self-esteem and social status. For this reason AT-T is a directive method. The Alpha psychotherapist directs the client's attention toward the more likely fear trigger scenarios and toward the most fear-inducing elements of those scenarios. As the therapist demonstrates accuracy in directing, and the client experiences the positive outcome of the Targeting intervention, the client becomes more trusting and feels safer during sessions.

The Therapist assists the client in recognizing that it is their fear that causes their anger. "She is such a nasty bitch!" really means she poses a threat to my self-esteem, which is why, "She makes me so angry!" really means, "She scares me!" which really means, "She reminds me of how weak, alone and not in control I feel!"

Eventually, however, the client's pleasure/pain principle will begin to function on a more human level. The client becomes more insightful and sensitive to the plights of others, and correspondingly more tolerant and patient. The client is not necessarily aware of this improvement unless it is brought to his or her attention. This is because a large part of being self-confident is not being so preoccupied with one's personal assets or needs. Deciphering the lessons inherent in life experiences begins to seem more interesting and more satisfying than physical and ego satisfactions. This means the instinct to seek pleasure and to avoid pain is beginning to function on a more human, less animal, level.

The following list of search areas can be used as guides to begin the process of identifying fear triggers in a variety of areas. The same or similar fear triggers apply in nearly all the areas. This is obviously because most fear triggers are fundamentally self-esteem issues, and the F-or-F feelings are the reaction of the experiencer. But since individuals tend to perceive their problems in the context of their own seemingly unique circumstances, a guide that seems to address their specific concerns can be helpful.

Clinicians and non-clinicians are free to make as many copies of these packets as needed for themselves, for friends or for use in individual and group therapy sessions, and they can be given to clients as free handouts.

Packet #1: Learning to Analyze Your Anger

Think back over the past week or two and remember all the times you became angry at someone or at something. Now list the fear trigger(s) that were the real reason your anger defense mechanism became active in each situation. It is not necessary to explain the whole set of circumstances, or whether it was partly or even totally your fault; just mentally picture the detail of the event that triggered one or more of your fear feelings. If you are making a list of fear triggers you identified during the day, keep it brief. You are not telling a story; use just enough description so you will remember what to mentally picture when you are ready to apply the Targeting intervention. Remember, your mental picture of the fear trigger is like pushing the Pause button on a VCR; picture it like a moment frozen in time. When a fear reaction is neutralized, any associated anger will go away by itself!

1. What someone did or said, or something that happened, that scared me (and I got angry).
2. What someone did or said, or something that happened, that embarrassed me (and I got angry).
3. What someone did or said, or something that happened, that disappointed me (and I got angry).
4. What someone did or said, or something that happened, that worried me (and I got angry).
5. What someone did or said, or something that happened, that hurt my feelings (and I got angry).

6. What someone did or said, or something that happened, that made me feel sad (and I got angry).
7. What someone did or said, or something that happened, that made me feel guilty or ashamed (and I got angry).

Get the idea? You should be able to list a fear trigger on just one line.

Then apply the AT-T intervention to each of the items on each of your lists, using Chapter Seven as a guide.

Packet #2: Dissatisfaction with Body Image

In privacy remove your clothing and stand in front of a full-length mirror. List on a piece of paper everything about your body that you dislike, think is flawed, worry about, wish were different, etc. No matter how trivial or silly it might seem, make a note of it anyway. Put your clothes back on and then perform the AT-T intervention on each listed item individually. When you do so, mentally picture each item in an exaggerated form, as if it were a major obstacle to your success in life or to your acceptance by peers. This exaggeration often makes it easier for you to notice which fear emotions you felt.

SOME POSSIBILITIES:

1. Hair: wrong color, too wavy, too straight, too dry, unmanageable, etc.
2. Skin: too white, too brown, too black, too coarse, too wrinkled, too dry, too sweaty, etc.
3. Body: too tall, too short, too fat, too plump, too skinny, too flabby, too weak, not muscular, poor posture, buttocks shaped wrong, bowlegged, ugly feet, etc.
4. Sexual organs: too big, too small, bad odor, wrong shape, too sweaty, too dry, looks wrong, looks ugly, too much pubic hair, not enough pubic hair, not sexually responsive enough, too sexually responsive, etc.

5. Ethnic: look too Asian, look too African, look too Hispanic, look too Arabic, look too Caucasian/white, look too Native American, look too foreign, etc.

Then apply the AT-T intervention—see Chapter Seven—individually on each item on each of your lists. When you mentally visualize each flaw—fear trigger—imagine each of them as very serious; exaggerate the "flaw," mentally picture it as interfering with your right or your ability to be successful and happy.

Packet #3: Academic Fear Triggers

Since the part of the brain that reacts with the F-or-F emotions does not recognize a "time line," fear triggers associated with education will be in the past, in the present and in the imagined future.

1. PAST: List all your memories of people, things and situations that troubled you in the classroom, at recess, going to and from school, social acceptance or rejection and when working on assignments either at home or at school.
2. PRESENT: List all the people, things and situations about education that seem to be worrying you right now —or these days—or causing you to hesitate or procrastinate or to have doubts about your ability, or get you to wondering whether what you are currently doing is good enough or is even worth the trouble.
3. FUTURE: List all the people, things and situations— whether real or imaginary—that make you feel even slightly uncomfortable about the prospect of continuing your education. *Let your imagination go on this one; mentally picture that WHAT COULD GO WRONG WILL GO WRONG!*

NOTE: When you apply the AT-T intervention—see Chapter Seven—on each item of the above three lists, mentally picture each one as very serious and extremely unpleasant, and potentially able to interfere with your ability to be successful in your future education and happy and successful in life.

Packet #4: Sports Performance Fear Triggers

All fear triggers have the effect of undermining performance and self-confidence as well as self-esteem. Part of the reason many athletes have occasional runs of poor performance is because they have perceived someone, something or some situation that was a fear trigger, which undermined their self-esteem, their self-confidence and subsequently their performance. Furthermore, they will most likely not be consciously aware of the real reason for their poor performance.

With the assistance of an AT-T therapist, the best solution will be to recall the unpleasant person or unpleasant situation that immediately preceded the decline in your performance. This does not mean the original imprinted paradigm in your childhood, although that would be the original cause. Instead, scan for the unpleasant experience that more recently preceded the drop in your performance and your self-confidence, possibly something that you shrugged off or barely even noticed at the time.

If you cannot recall when or how it started, the AT-T psychotherapist can assist you in performing the AT-T intervention on your immediate performance concerns of the day. This will produce the immediate effect of restoring your usual higher level of performance

For the purpose of examples, though, consider:

BASEBALL: Not on the starting lineup; missing a fly ball: getting hit in the face by a grounder; making a bad throw; walking too many batters; striking out; popping out; committing an error, etc.

BASKETBALL: Not on the starting lineup; missing a foul shot; missing a lay in; missing a shot of any kind; having the ball stolen from you; unnecessary fouling an opponent; traveling; bad pass; etc.

FOOTBALL: Not on the starting lineup; missing a block; fear of being sacked; throwing a bad pass; missing a pass; fumbling the ball; being pulled by the coach; bad place kick; etc.

SOCCER: Not on the starting lineup; called for off sides; being red tagged or yellow tagged; having the ball stolen; missing a goal-on kick opportunity; letting an opponent score on you; etc.

Then apply the AT-T intervention—see Chapter Seven—individually to each item on each of your lists, mentally picturing them as seriously bad experiences actually happening to you right now.

Packet #5: Sexual Fear Triggers— Gay, Lesbian, Bisexual & Heterosexual

Regardless of sexual orientation, sexual fear triggers tend to be universal, although they vary somewhat from person to person. They also vary in the kind of fear feelings triggered and in their relative intensity. Once sexual fears are resolved via the AT-T intervention there is no "Wow!" experience. Sexuality simply becomes less stressful, more natural in the context of one's sexual orientation, more pleasant, more reality-based and less fantasy-based. It is not a matter of what you or your partner do or do not do; rather, it is the stress-free communication and the development of mutually sufficient and satisfactory sexual interaction that evolves after the fear triggers have been neutralized.

Here are some typical fears:

Do I look okay; do I smell okay; am I doing what my partner wants; is my partner satisfied or disappointed; can I tell my partner what I like or don't like; should I initiate sex; how do I initiate sex; do I want sex too often; do I not want sex often enough; should I try new things; will my partner be disappointed if I try something new; is it okay if I say I don't feel like having sex right now; is my partner getting tired of me; did I offend my partner; is my partner interested in someone else?

Then apply the AT-T intervention—see Chapter Seven—individually to each of the items on your list, mentally picturing each of them in an exaggerated fashion, and as true.

Packet #6: Acceptance vs. Rejection Fear Triggers

Self-esteem and the sense of social status are closely interrelated. Most all people are almost constantly scanning the apparent attitudes, body language, facial expressions and remarks of others that might indicate degrees of acceptance or rejection. Besides these being unreliable indicators, this almost constant scanning for indications of social status is a terribly wasteful and unnecessary use of one's energy and consciousness. Use this guide to identify fear triggers associated with your excessive concerns about acceptance and rejection.

1. List all your memories of being rejected, disliked, disapproved of, unwelcome, just tolerated—or at least when you thought so.

2. List all the clues or hints or indications that you might not currently be as accepted, recognized, listened to or appreciated as you would like to be. Don't be concerned about whether you are being accurate or that you are being overly picky. If the thought pops into your mind, it is quite likely a legitimate fear trigger.

3. List all the people, situations, and any personal shortcomings—whether real or imagined—that could possibly put your acceptance, recognition, approval, etc., at risk. Use your imagination, but list things that could conceivably happen to you, however unlikely.

4. Now perform the AT-T intervention—see Chapter Seven—on each item on each of your lists, mentally picturing each unpleasant experience as happening to you right now. Do each item individually. After you have completed this packet, wait for

a week or so, and then do the packet again. You might find there are fear triggers that you were unable to recognize until you got the first level of fear triggers out of the way.

Packet #7: Self-Confidence & Self-Esteem Fear Triggers

This packet is to guide you in identifying personal things about yourself that until now you have tried to hide from other people, or even from yourself. Unless you can be truly open to the process of getting rid of your fear triggers, this can be a rather difficult and unpleasant packet to complete. But the payoff in increased self-esteem, self-confidence and assertiveness, as well as a higher functioning IQ will be well worth it!

1. List all the things about your body that you wish were better or different. *List everything, no matter how silly, dumb or trivial it might seem.* It can be helpful when doing this packet to imagine yourself naked and that people are observing how flawed you are.

2. List all the times you thought you embarrassed yourself, or at least you were worried that you looked or sounded like a know-it-all, a dodo, socially inept, stupid, a fool, and so on. Think about past social situations, classrooms, dates, on the job, etc.

3. List all the negative things people have said to you or about you, even if they were supposedly just joking. List all the criticisms, all the insults, all the teasing, and so on. This will include comments about how you were dressed, the car you drove, how you looked, how you have talked, how you have acted, your thoughts, how you have socialized, how you have played sports or a game, how you have responded to insults or criticisms, and so on.

4. Now apply the AT-T intervention—see Chapter Seven—to each of the items on each of your lists, mentally picturing each one as real and true.

The principle here is that you—as all people do—have secret concerns that you are not good enough, that you are somehow a flawed individual. Understand that wherever you are, whatever you are doing, you worry that your "flaws" prevent you from feeling truly welcome or from doing anything well enough, no matter what it is. This is the result of an imprinted paradigm from early childhood. It's not necessary or helpful for you to identify that paradigm or identify which adult was responsible for imprinting it. As you identify the fear triggers that directly interfere with your sense of personal value, the paradigm that caused them is weakened and your natural sense of self-esteem is restored.

Packet #8: Racial, Ethnic & Gender Fear Triggers

There has never been a time in recorded history when issues of racial, ethnic and gender inferiority/superiority have not been a problem. Wars and other forms of horrendous abuse have occurred over such issues. Problems associated with, "My race or ethnicity is better than yours!" "My gender is the best or the smartest!" are still causing serious problems all over the world. These cultural issues are not going to stop being a problem any time soon. Individually, though, they can be largely resolved, regardless of your race, ethnicity or gender.

This packet can guide you in identifying the fear triggers resulting from your imprinted racial/ethnic/gender paradigms. You are likely imprinted with paradigms that contain beliefs and expectations dictating that you are inferior as well as that you are superior. Let yourself recognize that you do have inflexible racial/ethnic/gender beliefs and expectations about yourself and about others that are contradictory, or simply wrong. Note: A paradigm that your race, ethnic origin or gender is superior is clearly not in your best interests because such imprints are inflexible, and based on imprint, not fact. They leave no room for learning, personal growth or the development of wisdom. In order to unburden yourself from these self-limiting and self-defeating imprints:

1. List all the racial or ethnic beliefs or expectations—even if you're not sure—that come to mind when you think of your own race or ethnic origin or those of anyone else. *List everything that comes to mind, even if you intellectually recognize it as stupid, trivial, untrue, just a stereotype, or whatever.* List it even if it was originally intended as just a joke. Don't leave out anything. If it pops into your mind it is probably a legitimate fear trigger. Get rid of it!

2. List every unpleasant experience you have ever had, or observed that someone else had, regardless of why, that you believe was directly or indirectly related to your race, ethnic origin or gender, or related to someone else's race, ethnic origin or gender. Include related scenes of cruelty or unfairness that bothered you in movies.

3. List anything directly or indirectly related to your—or someone else's—race, ethnic origin or gender that might make you feel unsure of yourself, make you want to leave, make you feel angry or cause you to feel any fear emotion, or combination of fear emotions. Include anything that could conceivably occur in school, on the job, during a job interview, at the mall, in a store, in church, synagogue, temple, masjid, on TV or in a movie, or in any social situation.

4. Now, identify the detail(s) in each situation you listed that is—or are—the actual fear trigger(s). These will be the details that made the situation memorable to you as you made your list.

5. Then, individually apply the AT-T intervention—see Chapter Seven—to each item on each of your lists, mentally picturing each one as if it were truly happening to you right now.

Packet #9: Spiritual & Religious Fear Triggers

1. List your spiritual or religious beliefs, even if you're not sure about them.

2. List spiritual or religious beliefs that you think are different from yours, even if you're not sure.

3. List any spiritual or religious beliefs that you have heard of that have disturbed you.

4. Then apply the AT-T intervention—see Chapter Seven—to each belief listed that makes you even *slightly* uncomfortable, mentally picturing each one as a serious and very troubling issue for you right now.

Packet #10: Death & Dying Fear Triggers

1. List the unpleasant ways you could truly imagine yourself dying some day.

2. List all the reasons you can imagine that could make being dead unpleasant.

3. Then, individually apply the AT-T intervention—see Chapter Seven—to each of these unpleasant mental pictures, mentally picturing each one as a very unpleasant personal reality that is happening to you right now.

NOTE: Don't avoid listing anything because it seems silly or unlikely; if you thought of it, it probably is a fear trigger!

Packet #11: Illness Fear Triggers

1. List all the illnesses you have worried about or that you would dread having.

2. List all the more unpleasant or painful illnesses you've read about, seen in pictures or seen others have.

3. Then apply the AT-T intervention—see Chapter Seven—individually to each illness, mentally picturing yourself as if you are suffering from it right now.

Packet #12: Aging & Old Age Fear Triggers

Note: This packet will probably better address the fear triggers of someone who is middle-aged or older. Otherwise, it's for anyone who has concerns in this area.

1. List all the details about yourself that show you are getting old.

2. List all the things about old people that you find unpleasant or unattractive.

3. List how *bad* you might look when you get *really old*.

4. List all the things younger people might find unpleasant or unattractive about you because you are *too old*.

5. Then individually apply the AT-T intervention—see Chapter Seven—to each item on all four lists, picturing them as applying to you right now.

Packet #13: Marriage Fear Triggers

This packet can be used to address premarital issues or existing marital issues.

1. PREMARITAL: List every reason you can think of to avoid marriage, or to cancel your existing commitment to get married. List everything, even if it seems trivial, childish, or unreasonable.

2. PREMARITAL: List everything about your intended that isn't exactly the way you would like, no matter how trivial, unrealistic, unreasonable or unfair of you.

3. MARITAL: List everything you think your spouse or partner might not like about you or about your relationship.

4. Then, individually apply the AT-T intervention—see Chapter Seven—to each item on each list, mentally picturing each one as a serious and very unpleasant issue that is a problem right now.

Packet #14: Child-Rearing Fear Triggers

1. List all the reasons, no matter how trivial, that you think means you are not a very good parent.

2. List all the reasons your child (or children) might resent you or disapprove of you as a parent.

3. List all your fears or worries, no matter how unrealistic or unlikely, about how your child—or children—might turn out or what they might do.

4. Then, individually apply the AT-T intervention—see Chapter Seven—to each item on each list, mentally picturing your worst fears have come true.

Packet #15: Job & Career Fear Triggers

1. List all the things that might be indications that you are not doing a very good job. Don't leave anything out just because it might seem trivial, unimportant, or foolish.

2. List all the reasons you think your employer might wish you did not work for him or her. Again, don't leave anything out just because it might seem trivial, unimportant or foolish, or overly suspicious on your part.

3. List all the indications that could mean that your co-workers don't like working with you. Again, list every little detail no matter what it is.

4. Then, individually apply the AT-T intervention—see Chapter Seven—to each item on all three lists, mentally picturing each one as if it were true.

Packet #16: Alien Encounter & Abduction Fear Triggers

This writer has never knowingly had a personal encounter with aliens or personally observed what was thought to be a UFO. But to a competent Alpha psychotherapist, a personal belief or lack of belief in such things is not relevant to the therapy process. The various forms of fear are very real to the client, and it is the job of the Alpha psychotherapist to assist in disconnecting the client's fears from whatever triggers them.

1. FEAR OF BEING ABDUCTED: List everything you have thought about, seen, read or heard about that you hope will never happen to you.

2. FEAR OF BEING ABDUCTED: List things you have never actually heard or read about, but that you hope will never happen to you. List anything that pops into your mind, no matter how silly or unlikely it might seem as you write it on the list.

3. BEEN ABDUCTED: List every unpleasant alien-related experience you have had. Don't skip anything just because you are not sure it happened the way you remember it, or because you think maybe you just dreamed it, or because of whatever other doubts you might have—or other people might have—about the reality of those experiences.

4. Then, individually apply the AT-T intervention—see Chapter Seven—to each item on each of your lists, mentally picturing each one as a serious problem right now.

Remember, don't expect a WOW! experience to result from the Alpha Therapy-Targeting intervention. The only change will be that the fear triggers you have targeted will never be fear triggers for you again.

Chapter Seven
How to Do the AT-T Intervention

Power/Control (Fight Feelings)			Security/Safety (Flight Feelings)		
Bored	Frustrated	Angry	Nervous	Sad	Scared
Disdainful	Indignant	Furious	Afraid	Guilty	Disappointed
Impatient	Hostile	Enraged	Worry	Envious	Terrified
Annoyed	Resentful	Hateful	Anxious	Panicky	Embarrassed
Irritated		Mad	Hurt		Horrified

Avoid slang terms like "ticked off," "pissed," "bitter," or blaming terms like "humiliated," "cheated," "rejected," etc. Use the feeling words listed above; their meanings are clear and unambiguous and they don't usually change with social trends. Keep it clear and simple so your nervous system understands.

Use about 7 different AFFIRMATION PHRASES (repeated 10 times) for each target!

1. It's okay to be me.	10. I don't have to be like him (her).
2. I am enough.	11. I don't have to prove anything.
3. It's okay when I don't know what to do.	12. I don't have to please him (her).
4. I can be patient.	13. I don't have to fear criticism.
5. I am beautiful, capable and lovable.	14. I don't have to feel guilty.
6. I am not afraid.	15. I don't have to be afraid.
7. It's okay if he (or she) says that.	16. I don't have to be angry.
8. It's okay if he (or she) does that.	17. I don't have to be perfect.
9. It's okay if he (or she) is that way.	18. I don't have to pretend.

The only difficult part of the AT-T intervention is identifying the *real reasons* you get so angry, the *real reasons* you don't speak up in a meeting or social group, the *real reasons* you don't set goals, the *real reasons* you don't ask for help. Can you recognize the fears that activate your anger, the fears that weaken your self-confidence, the fears that make you so critical?

To get good results you must have a good Target. A good Target is a mental picture of what hurt, shamed, disappointed or embarrassed you, or will unless you stay away from it. A good Target is like a moment "frozen" in time, either in the past or in the imagined—feared!—future.

The AT-T intervention: Close your eyes and picture in your mind the worst part of what happened, or the worst part of what you imagine might happen. Notice the mild fear-type feelings triggered by just picturing it! Then, open your eyes and choose an Affirmation Phrase from the menu. Re-close your eyes and *silently, mentally* repeat it ten times, placing emphasis on a different word each time—For example: **I** am enough!, I **am** enough!, I am

enough!, **I** am enough!, I **am** enough!, I am **enough**!. Open your eyes only to choose another Affirmation Phrase, then re-close them. You will probably forget to mentally picture the fear trigger once you begin repeating the Affirmation Phrases. Don't worry, the intervention will still work. It only matters that you first opened the emotional wound by mentally picturing the fear trigger, noted the fear feelings and their location in your body. If someone or something interrupts you before you begin repeating the Affirmation Phrases, it's a good idea to re-start the AT-T intervention by mentally re-picturing the fear trigger.

Anger hides your fear feelings, gives you a false sense of power and control and makes you think your angry words or actions are justified. Internal anger makes you critical of people and critical of situations, as well as causing you to make foolish or self-limiting decisions. Do you still trust your own anger? Do you still trust angry people? Of course you don't!

Chapter Eight
AT-T and Sports Performance

COMPETITIVE SPORTS INVARIABLY TRIGGER emotional stress which is, of course, the player's instinctive Fight-or-Flight (F-or-F) response to real or imagined threats to self-esteem and/or social status. These fear and anger responses are always counterproductive because they are emotions dedicated to energizing the athlete to either fight or to run away, neither of which is acceptable. Both fear and anger interfere with the athlete's focus on the task at hand and with his or her athletic skills. Depending upon the seriousness and the intensity of early childhood negative imprinting, the F-or-F emotions activated during a contest might linger for a few minutes, for the remainder of the contest, for the entire season, or for an entire athletic career.

Remember, anger is a defense mechanism that enables the athlete to be less aware of whatever fear feelings are associated with the threat; i.e., anger feels better than fear. An athlete's anger or resentment will remain—seemingly to ward off the threat to self-esteem—as long as the threat remains emotionally unresolved, even when he or she is not consciously thinking about it.

The athlete whose anger lingers on is unknowingly exercising a need to remain unaware of the threat to self-esteem and social status. This athlete might be grumpy, might engage in rude humor that is hurtful to others, have a blunted sense of humor, resent being disagreed with, behave arrogantly toward teammates, break team rules, resent constructive criticism, engage in especially crude trash talk, become abusive toward their spouse, complain about and question coaching, commit more fouls or errors, gravitate socially toward teammates with similar attitudes, isolate socially from teammates, be self-medicating with drugs or alcohol, and the list goes on. This athlete's performance might be inconsistent, excellent one game then poor the next.

The angry athlete is sometimes too threatened by self-esteem fears to be able to even consider the possibility that their anger is fear-based. If there is a strongly imprinted belief that it is unacceptable to show fear or to admit to fear, then any suggestion to the contrary can actually trigger a new and greater fear, that of decompensation. To put it more clearly, the athlete might have a fear of breaking down and crying, which he or she likely believes would be a major threat to self-esteem. It is unlikely that true decompensation—the exacerbation of symptoms of a preexisting disorder—would actually occur, but this athlete's fear of it strengthens his or her internal, unconscious commitment to denial. This would indicate the existence of a strongly imprinted inflexible paradigm from early childhood. Most angry athletes are not so severely locked into denial of fear, though, and would be able to respond eventually to a skilled Alpha psychotherapist. The athlete who is aware that some forms of fear are involved will not usually display lasting anger, if any at all, toward what was considered the threat to self-esteem.

However, even this athlete might become more easily drawn into a conflict of mutual arrogance with a teammate, in which he or she might temporarily display impatience, frustration, annoyance, disdain, etc., all the milder forms of anger. Such conflicts are often resolvable because this athlete realizes to some degree that the peer conflict stems from self-esteem fears relative to personal performance and that the conflict is partly a facade.

The athlete who is consciously burdened with performance fear is at greater risk for developing what might be called a "loop" of negative expectation. Put simply, the athlete performs poorly and then obsessively worries that the poor performance will be repeated. This imagery, usually referred to as worry, increases the likelihood that the poor performance will in fact be repeated. Probably all athletes have experienced such loops. Most recover from them after a short time, but some have had to endure them for whole seasons or for their entire careers. These loops of fear-based negative expectation can be resolved easily and quickly with AT-T.

Another kind of loop of negative expectation commonly occurs with athletes. This loop often occurs immediately after the athlete has performed exceptionally well in a recent contest. The more outstanding the level of performance, sometimes the worse the loop of negative expectation will be. By their recent display of excellence, they have demonstrated to everyone what they are capable of doing. This athlete begins to obsessively worry—mentally picture—that in the next contest he or she will revert to a lower level of performance, or worse, and that everyone will then be disappointed.

Sometimes an athlete's loop is tied into a more insidious imprint—inflexible paradigm imprinted in early childhood—about there being an unknown inherently "fatal flaw" that will inevitably interfere with any hopes of continuing success in sports, or in any other endeavor. In fact many individuals, not just athletes, suffer from various kinds of "fatal flaw" imprints.

The athlete who is consciously aware of feeling fear can usually be encouraged to develop mental pictures—Targets—of past fear-producing performance experiences as well as anticipated ones, which serve as very effective and beneficial targets for AT-T. By constructing mental images—Targets—that exemplify "worst possible scenarios" of "what are the worst things that could possibly happen?" the athlete can use the AT-T intervention to neutralize most of the real or imaginary reasons to be afraid.

Chapter Nine
AT-T and Religion and Spirituality

REPETITION HAS HISTORICALLY PLAYED A MAJOR role in the teaching and practices of all religions. Very early cultures were aware that repetition can enhance learning and recall, whether this was realized via early scientific observation, through intuition, or perhaps by accident. For centuries, religious people have used this technique. First the individual would acknowledge a problem, then follow with monotonous repetition of a prayer or a spiritual mantra, in an effort to produce some kind of resolution of the problem. The most common pattern is something along the lines of "I am a sinner!" immediately followed by mental or verbal repetitions of "Lord, have mercy and forgive me!" Variations on this theme have been used in most all religions, and continue to this day. They provide just enough monotony to induce Alpha brain wave dominance.

It is really quite simple. Repetition of any kind eventually becomes monotonous. If it produces mild monotony contiguous to—immediately following—the mental picturing of a problem or concern, it induces a potentially insight-producing ratio of Beta and Alpha brain waves. We know this ratio to be Alpha wave dominant, instead of the usual environment-attentive Beta wave dominance. Beta wave activity—the so-called wide-awake state of consciousness—enables a person to be aware of sensory information: tastes, smells, sounds, visual observations and physical sensations. The reticular system in your brain filters out information that seems less interesting—though not necessarily less important!

Nonetheless, most of the time individuals are outwardly focused—Beta brain wave dominant. Increased Beta wave activity, in addition to enabling an individual to be aware mostly of sensory perception, is also associated with thinking that is linear, logical, practical, numerical, etc. Beta waves also enable you to be aware of external information such as peer pressure, social expectations, the demands of imprinted spiritual values, compliments and criticisms, and so on. It is noteworthy that the fight-or-flight emotions—degrees of anger and various types of fear—are more likely to be active in association with Beta brain wave dominance.

In contrast, Alpha brain waves enable you to be more inwardly focused, as in spiritual reverie, imagining, daydreaming, wondering, contemplating, artistically/creatively thinking, globally/integratively thinking, intuitively thinking and philosophically thinking. This is an oversimplification of how the brain waves work, but it is sufficient for the purpose of understanding AT-T. It is also sufficient for an understanding of why repetition has historically been a primary methodology of religions and of education of all kinds.

Most religions encourage the repetition of certain phrases or words. Usually they are clearly spiritual, such as, "Lord, have mercy; Christ, have mercy," "Om Sri Sai Ram," "Hare Krishna," "Om mane padme hum," the rosary, etc. There are probably hundreds of thousands of such phrases in different languages and religions, all of which are for the purpose of increasing an individual's religious or spiritual awareness.

Religions still use a variety of techniques in an effort to induce the optimal mix of Alpha and Beta brain waves—again, whether accidentally or by the conscious intent of religious leaders. Special atmosphere is created with dim lights, bright lights, candles, incense, icons and statues, altars and various rituals. In these specialized atmospheres, there is often repetitious prayer, chanting, readings and ceremonial activity, conducted by a leader who is usually ceremonially attired.

Those attending religious rituals are there because of their imprinted beliefs about personal obligation, spiritual atonement and devotional obligations, as well as the hope and expectation that their attendance will somehow alleviate their sense of being inherently imperfect or incomplete—also the result of early childhood imprinted paradigms. Most all "belief systems" are imprinted during early childhood and are psychologically recognized as rigid, inflexible paradigms. Most people consider the ups and downs of ordinary life experiences to somehow be "proof" that their spiritual beliefs—paradigms—are correct, regardless of what form their spiritual beliefs have.

The psychological analysis of spiritual beliefs and practices need not detract from their validity. There is far too much unexplainable evidence of their effectiveness to even consider calling them into question. No science, certainly not the science of psychology, can legitimately challenge spiritual enlightenment, God-consciousness, transcendental awareness, the supernatural, and so on. There is no need to challenge them. Which religious or spiritual imprinted paradigms are right and which are wrong, whether all of them are right or all of them are wrong, is not what this chapter is about. The problem with all imprinted paradigms, spiritual or otherwise, is their inflexibility. Their inflexibility is what interferes with learning, change and personal growth, even in spiritual matters.

When one enters a temple, mosque, masjid, church or synagogue, one certainly does not leave one's personal paradigms at the door! Each of us is to some degree burdened to the extent that our beliefs are rigid and inflexible. This applies just as much to individuals who have "converted" to a different religion or to a different set of spiritual beliefs. An individual who converts to another religion tends to transfer their personal paradigms from one belief system to the other. Members of a convert's previous religion tend to view the convert as having "fallen"; members of the religion receiving the individual tend to view the convert as having "risen." The convert might be happier and feel more grounded. But psychologically, it can be likened to a beneficial career change.

Most actively religious people focus primarily on the more peripheral aspects of their particular religion, such as tithing, social activities, charities, ceremonies, etc., all of which are defensible values. What tends to be ignored—by regular members as well as by the convert—however, are the beliefs, expectations and guidance at the heart of most religions that are supposed to direct individuals toward the achievement of some kind of ultimate spiritual transcendence.

This is exciting stuff! Individuals who have seemingly achieved "spiritual transcendence" stand out as truly incredible role models, apparently unlimited by what science assumes are natural laws! Why are people not rushing to take advantage of what appears to be such an incredible opportunity? A large part of this lack of motivation is very likely due to an imprinted sense of personal unworthiness and the imprinted paradigms that dictate material acquisition, social recognition, the denial of fear and the appearance of being already sufficiently self-assured.

There are likely some unavoidable steps on the path toward the goal of spiritual transcendence. The individual will no doubt have to face his or her personal fears and make them disappear, not by denial or by hiding them, but by somehow neutralizing them and recognizing that they were irrelevant, without substance, an illusion. Being told this by some highly trusted mentor will not make it so. Each individual must experience their own personal transition from the illusion that their fears and their anger are externally "caused," and are "real," to knowing their fears and anger are animal-level defenses that are interfering with their humanity and their ability to look for something beyond their physical body and their social status.

Millions of people have been killed, injured, tortured, insulted and/or socially abused or rejected in the name of organized religions. It still goes on in the world, rivaling or at least equaling, racial prejudice in its intensity. This behavior, like racial prejudice, is largely the product of the imprinting of inflexible paradigms during early childhood. This is why there are no "good" imprinted paradigms.

AT-T can play a key role in the reduction of fear-sanctioned paradigms that can so limit one's self-esteem and personal growth. It can also eliminate one's perception of "other" religious beliefs as threats to one's own imprinted beliefs and expectations about how they themselves should be and how other people and the world around them should be. It is now possible to begin to overcome many of the fears that no doubt prevent individuals from perceiving themselves as worthy and capable of following through successfully with whatever discipline it takes to attain a spiritual goal they had thought was beyond their reach.

If you would like to clear out some of your fear triggers in this area, in Chapter Six you will find *Packet #9, Spiritual and Religious Fear Triggers.* It will provide some guidance in identifying some details of your own religious beliefs that worry you a little, as well as some "other" beliefs that worry you a little. Remember, fear is the enemy, not other people's spiritual beliefs. If you take advantage of this opportunity—and I think most everyone should!—you will probably be surprised that you have been burdened with so many fear triggers pertaining to your own religious beliefs—or lack thereof—as well as pertaining to those of other people.

You see, you won't know you have an inflexible paradigm about religion or spirituality until you notice that you feel a little troubled—or maybe a lot troubled—by someone, by something, or by an idea that seems to be in contradiction to how you think it should be. Hopefully, you will realize how frequently you have indulged in devaluing thoughts about those "other" religious beliefs, those "other" people, and those "other" religious practices.

How can you tell when you are mostly free of inflexible religious and spiritual paradigms? The first clue is that you are no longer personally troubled—you feel little or no fear or anger—when you encounter beliefs that are very different from or contradictory to your beliefs. Instead, you are either benignly disinterested or you experience a curiosity to know more about them and perhaps a desire to understand them and their origin in more detail. The normal, healthy individual is not locked into a belief system that considers different belief systems as demonic or something to be avoided.

Many religions have a few members who are so narrow and fundamentalist that they believe they have a "divine" right to attack, any way they can, others who have different beliefs. Such individuals are often considered "outlaws" and an embarrassment by the more balanced members of that religion. When a person therapeutically applies AT-T to their own fear triggers they become more able to differentiate among the potentially dangerous members of their own religion as well as the potentially dangerous members of other religions. They are able to recognize that the potentially dangerous individuals do not truly or accurately reflect the values of whichever religion they claim. Such militants are recognized as being burdened with dangerous negative paradigms which actually have no basis in religion or spirituality.

Chapter Ten
AT-T and Minority Fears

THROUGHOUT HISTORY THERE HAVE BEEN GROUPS of people designated by the locally dominant population as inferior. The negative effects of these "we're better than you" systems have ranged from social ostracism to slavery to a horrible process called "ethnic cleansing." Such severely dysfunctional social systems often seem to have originated out of competition over territorial and economic acquisition and fundamentalist religious beliefs as well as ethnic differences.

As the world moves forward with increased communication, increased information, increased travel and more interconnected economics, the idea of one population designating themselves as inherently superior to another population has fallen into disrepute. Attempting to maintain overt dominance over a minority of people in this manner is becoming recognized worldwide as distasteful and culturally backward.

In spite of changing attitudes, this social dysfunction still exists in varying degrees throughout the world. Children born into the dominant population are imprinted with prejudicial values and attitudes. They are often unaware that they possess such prejudices and will innocently deny having them when asked. Depending upon the strength of their imprinted paradigms, those individuals who are aware of their prejudices might tend to consider them justifiable, even though they cannot explain how. In fact, they often do not think of them as prejudices, but as reality based values, no matter how illogical or ridiculous.

But what of those individuals who have been born into a long-standing tradition of being the ethnic, religious or cultural objects of prejudice? What kinds of imprints might they have received while very young? Under such conditions one can assume dominated minority parents would teach their children to avoid the wrath of members of the dominant population. Parents who have long since accepted the inevitability of a lifetime of second class, or worse, citizenship serve unwittingly as role models for their children. Their children, like children everywhere, see their parents as normal and by their example they are imprinted with the adaptive attitudes—imprinted paradigms—modeled by their parents. They are unknowingly imprinted with a dysfunctional self-esteem that blends with the dysfunctional social system. These children unwittingly help to perpetuate the dysfunctional social system because they are unaware of their imprinted dysfunctional self-esteem paradigm, and are therefore not inclined to overcome their predicament.

It feels safer, and therefore more comfortable, to remain in the social role of second-class citizen. They are free to enjoy the illusions of empowerment and of being in control by criticizing and blaming the dominant population for being so insensitive and uncaring—but only when it seems safe to be so outspokenly critical. To many minority individuals, this gives them the illusion of having the moral right to disregard the laws and mores of the dominant population. It is not difficult to understand how an abused minority might not consider themselves morally obligated to respect the rules or laws promulgated by an abusive majority, whether the abuse occurs in economic, ethnic or religious areas.

This is arguably a nearly unavoidable adjustment on the part of any abused minority, given an essentially inescapable and hopelessly dysfunctional social system. After a few generations it becomes overly accepted by both the disenfranchised and the entitled, both groups having been imprinted from childhood with the cultural habit of going along with the status quo. Yet, neither social group is happy with the status quo. In fact, schools have been placing increasing emphasis on the social concept of equality and social justice. Racial, ethnic, religious and gender prejudice are becoming overtly unpopular. But children continue to be negatively imprinted with the myth of superiority versus inferiority and continue to perpetuate the problem; the oppressed minority have become passive/aggressive, almost unconsciously, in expressing their dislike for the ways they are mistreated or ignored.

Under the existing circumstances not very much can be done to alleviate the situation, since individuals in both populations were imprinted with their respective roles and attitudes as children. The self-entitled and the disenfranchised are equally trapped emotionally. This is true, unfortunately, in spite of some groups in each population who have become enlightened more rapidly than others in their respective populations.

The situation of a client born to a family that has for generations been subjected to prejudice—and probably still is—presents a unique and valuable opportunity for therapists who have the necessary skills. It probably has never been studied from the standpoint of neutralizing the fear triggers that accrue from this type of negative paradigms. The Western world has not, until recently, produced a method of psychotherapy that effectively addresses self-limiting and self-defeating fear triggers of any kind. The many categories of disadvantaged individuals throughout the world could be assisted in identifying the real as well as the imaginary fears that interfere with their self-esteem. Since it is not necessary to identify the original negative imprinting, it is not a particularly difficult task, using AT-T, to enable individual victims of social prejudice to begin to rediscover their natural self-esteem, given that they have access to an AT-T therapist and are willing and able to identify their fear triggers.

Now is a good time for therapists to take on the task of enabling members of the various minority groups to disconnect the imprinting that designates them in various ways as ugly, incompetent, unlovable and inherently flawed. Never before have there been methods so readily available—AT-T and EMDR—to begin to resolve these unique self-esteem issues. The individual willing to accept a therapist's help in this area will require exactly the same encouragement and support as would any client with emotional, behavioral or self-esteem problems.

Just as would any client, this client will need to experience the effectiveness of AT-T as it resolves "safer" fear issues, before getting to the more sensitive scenarios. This client will need to experience the therapist as a competent, caring and nonjudgmental guide in the search for fear triggers.

The client is encouraged to think about, and to visualize, the worst possible things about themselves. The client indulges in a kind of "creative negative thinking." This is not the usual concerns about peer disapproval or rejection. It is much more basic because it is more closely connected to imprinted negative paradigms dictating loyalty to ethnicity. It involves negative paradigms dictating loyalty to parents and extended family and to friends. It is the process of becoming conscious of the low opinion the client has of his or her ethnicity.

The client might sometimes feel like they are being ungrateful by acknowledging that their parents have passively accepted their second-class citizenship. If an ethnic minority client can get past all this by using AT-T, they will become able to understand that their parents had no choice in the matter. Neither AT-T nor EMDR were available to them. Such an understanding constitutes true forgiveness.

It is a complex set of scenarios, with as many variations as there are clients. The themes of prejudice are the same but each individual is uniquely imprinted, even within the same family, and each individual makes a slightly different adjustment to the social dysfunction into which they were born.

Chapter Eleven
AT-T and Academic Fears

EMOTIONAL STRESS IS CURRENTLY A VIRTUALLY unavoidable part of school and it interferes with student performance on all educational levels, from elementary school to graduate school. Everyone has experienced the stress associated with academic peer pressure, tests, exams and pop quizzes, being called on in the classroom, participation in classroom discussions, learning math concepts, foreign languages, science, time management, getting started on a term paper, homework, reading comprehension, writing skills, reading aloud and fear of possibly disappointing grades.

It is clearly understood that academic emotional stress is not inherent in any external events or experiences, but in one's fearful and sometimes angry responses to them. It is the real or imagined threats to one's self-esteem or to one's sense of social status, called fear triggers, that bring on the emotional stress response. One wonders why, knowing this, educators don't make changes in how educating is done, so as to minimize unnecessary fear triggers experienced by students so that they are better able to become educated. It is fairly well known that fear of any kind and anger in any degree of intensity interferes with one's functional intelligence and in one's performance.

The fact is high achieving students perform well in spite of their fears. Most students under-achieve to some degree, regardless of their grade point average (GPA). For some reason fear triggers were purposely introduced into the academic process hundreds of years ago. For unclear reasons, many educators still believe academic fear triggers are necessary in order to "weed out" those less motivated and to avoid making the acquisition of an education "too easy."

Also, students with a 4.0 GPA often display under-development in some non-academic areas, such as creative thinking, communication skills, social skills, self-confidence and group participation skills. Interestingly, if a student's imprinted negative paradigms from early childhood regarding academic success are less severe, their burden of academic expectations and the associated emotional stress is less severe and they also tend to have fewer shortcomings in non-academic areas.

For many students, however, the emotional stress of academics is significantly debilitating. Until the introduction of Alpha Therapy—and EMDR, if and when it is used to address academic fear triggers—there was little to be done about it other than the providing of encouragement and emotional support by family, teachers and friends, or in more severe cases, antidepressant medication. The added burden of learning disorders such as dyslexia or attention deficit disorder—ADD, or AD/HD when there is also hyperactivity—even if they are effectively medicated, sometimes compound a student's academic fear triggers.

Several areas should be reviewed by the AT-T psychotherapist and the student/client for potential fear triggers in order to enable him or her to more easily perform according to their natural academic potential. These include, but are not limited to, social situations, extracurricular activities, time management issues, leadership opportunities, test anxiety, and literally fear of the material being studied. *First*, the AT-T psychotherapist needs to address the immediate trouble spots, those that the student identifies as currently the most problematical. The student/client might assume much of his or her academic stress is simply par for the course. The AT-T psychotherapist needs to understand that there is nothing inherently fear provoking about education.

This is an opportunity for the student/client to experience the effectiveness of AT-T and to develop confidence in the therapist's ability to guide them in identifying and neutralizing academic fear triggers. The student/client describes recent events or situations that have made him or her feel any combination of fear feelings. He or she also describes academic situations that have not occurred, but were they to actually happen, would trigger fear responses of some kind. These anticipated disasters, even if rather unlikely, can be real possibilities that require pre-planning to be avoided, or, they can be almost absurd in their unlikelihood. Either way, they are unconsciously derived from the student's early childhood negative imprinted paradigms and are addressed via AT-T as if they were as real as any other fear trigger. Remember, regardless of what the fear trigger is the fear response is very real!

Second, the Alpha therapist directs the student/client to identify the belief—fear—that he or she lacks what other students seem to have, namely, the ability to be successful in various academic or school related areas. The student/client is struggling with imprinted unreasonable beliefs about their academic incompetence or unrealistic expectations about what they are supposed to achieve. As many of these self-limiting beliefs as possible are identified and treated via the AT-T intervention. With eyes closed, the student/client mentally pictures themselves failing horribly in a variety of school-related scenarios, one at a time. Each of these mental pictures is a fear trigger, and each is individually addressed via AT-T, and thereby neutralized. It is not necessary, and is usually not possible, to identify the original imprinting experience.

Third, the AT-T psychotherapist directs the student/client to identify their beliefs about being ugly, incompetent—or perhaps dumb or stupid—and unlovable. Such beliefs can cause the student/client to feel unworthy of academic success. Put differently, the student is struggling with early childhood negative paradigms that dictate unreasonable beliefs and expectations about how they are or should be, and unreasonable beliefs and expectations about how things are or should be and how other people are or should be.

The AT-T psychotherapist guides the student/client in addressing each fear trigger individually. Over a series of therapy sessions there is continual review of the targeted fear triggers to assess whether there are any other fear triggers in those areas already addressed. To assess outcome—see Chapter 15—the AT-T psychotherapist engages the student/client in the discussion of fear trigger scenarios already treated with the AT-T intervention. Of significance are facial expressions, body language, tone of voice, use of vocabulary, and any indications of blaming or justifying.

Due to the instinctive drive to seek comfort and to avoid discomfort, any client can occasionally fall into consciously or unconsciously avoiding an unpleasant topic by exaggerating how much improved they are. Under such circumstances the thought of attending another AT-T session might have become in itself a fear trigger. The psychotherapist might need to guide the student/client in targeting their fear of another therapy session, or even their fear of the AT-T psychotherapist.

Chapter Twelve
AT-T and Addiction Recovery Fears

THERE ARE AN ENDLESS VARIETY OF things and experiences to be addicted to besides alcohol and drugs. The list includes, but is not limited to, sex, TV, eating, pornography, masturbation, shopping, work, gambling, disagreeing and arguing, house cleaning, and the whole category of phobias, which, as far as AT-T is concerned, are rather like an addiction in reverse. The Alpha psychotherapist treats them all in the same way: with eyes closed, the client mentally pictures the fear trigger—whether it's a fear that something might happen, or a fear that something might not happen—identifies the fear-type feelings experienced by just mentally picturing the fear trigger; the client reports the fear sensations in the stomach area; then the AT-T intervention is applied.

Alcoholism, until around mid-century, was the classic addiction problem. Now heroin, cocaine and a variety of other so-called recreational drugs have become equally problematic. The Twelve Steps to Recovery, Alcoholics Anonymous (AA) and similar programs have been addressing alcohol abuse and drug abuse, and more recently, addictions to shopping, eating, sex, and several other areas of behavior.

Yet, many addicted individuals are not able to benefit from the above programs or else avoid them entirely. A common reason people avoid such recovery programs is because in order to benefit from them an addict or alcoholic must integrate them more or less permanently into their personal and social lifestyle. With some recovery programs an individual is required to have an outspoken dependency on a "higher power." Some individuals find they cannot internalize such a concept of a higher power in the required manner. In spite of their acknowledgment of the misery of addiction, many individuals find this requirement extremely unappealing.

In addition, even some recovered alcoholics sense there is something questionable about repeatedly admitting that in terms of their addiction they are "out of control" and "powerless to control their cravings." The philosophy of the programs, however, is that the inability of an addicted person to surrender to a "higher power" is indicative of the denial defense mechanism. Denial, the dreaded "D" word, is the response to anyone who is unsuccessful in these programs or any psychotherapist who even suggests there might be a better way to become and to remain sober. This observation will not be interpreted, I hope, as detracting from the value of these programs to those thousands of people who have benefited from them. But the fact is, almost any kind of program will work with about 25-30% of its participants, whether the program makes sense or not.

The fact is, strong advocates of The Twelve Steps and AA tend to suspect that any suggestion of a new method of recovery is simply a more sophisticated form of denial. Inevitably, though, as our knowledge and understanding of human psychology increases, promising new techniques and methodologies do emerge. One of these is Alpha Therapy-Targeting (AT-T). The current designation of alcoholism as a disease is seen by some as a reaction to the strong social prejudice that alcoholics could stop drinking if they just tried harder. While that might be true in some cases, a beneficial result of the disease designation is that it might have given some alcoholics a reason to join a recovery program without feeling like a weakling.

The disease designation cannot last much longer because the symptoms, however horrific in the case of alcoholism, apply equally to a huge variety of addictions to other things, as mentioned above. It wouldn't make much sense to designate pedophiles, for example, as victims of a disease. If society were to do so it could result in some very surprising and, unfortunately, successful conviction appeals. Alcoholism is often described as the persistent conscious desire for an alcoholic drink, and for its toxic effect. The obsessive thought process might occur on weekends, some evenings, daily, or just several times a year. There is no standard pattern of alcohol addiction, except that it seems to involve periodic obsessive imagery of drinking and an unrelenting desire to become intoxicated.

Pedophiles, sex addicts, food addicts, shopping addicts, TV addicts, etc., experience a similar pattern of obsessive mental images that gradually takes over much of their conscious lives. People who suffer from any of a variety of serious addictions tend to be treated with the same prejudice as alcoholics once were, as if they could refrain from engaging in such behavior if they would just try harder. I once interviewed a 70-year-old convict in a prison. He was back as a parole violator. I will always remember this old convict saying to me, with tears in his eyes, "If I could just stop thinking about it." He was referring to reaching under the dresses of little girls.

Alpha Therapy is not at all intended to replace The Twelve Steps or AA, or any other cognitive treatment methodology. What it does offer is a means of dealing more effectively with some inherent weaknesses in those programs. The inherent weakness of cognitive methods is that they are not designed to alleviate the fear-type feelings experienced when one denies oneself what one considers a particularly satisfying experience.

What Alpha Therapy provides is the permanent elimination, or at the very least the permanent significant and sufficient reduction, of those unpleasant feelings associated with self-denial.

Cognitive recovery programs like AA and The Twelve Steps require that the participant integrate the programs into their personal lifestyle for a very good reason. Participants attend meetings and socialize as often as possible with one another so as to maintain the external reinforcement to remain sober, drug-free, or free of whatever is their addiction. If the constant external support and reinforcement remains sufficiently strong, it is often able to counteract the recovering addict's obsessive mental images of the pleasure of indulging in the experience to which the person is addicted. The principle is the same as with all cognitive therapies. If the addict can be structured to maintain non-addict thinking for a long enough period of time—no one has any idea how long a period is required—eventually their emotions will begin to reinforce non-addict thinking instead of addict thinking.

Some addicts have become able to rationalized their substance abuse to the point where they are unable to recognize the pain they have caused themselves or their family and their friends, not to mention to the community. Cognitive programs that can make them aware of these realities are essential to some categories of addicts, particularly those who began their substance abuse at a young age. This is because alcohol or drug intoxication has interfered with their social learning, the development of a healthy sense of self and the development of a healthy sense of values.

Some Guidance in Identifying Addiction Fear Triggers

If you are a recovering addict, the following list of possible targets, though not all inclusive, provides examples of typical fear triggers a recovering alcohol or drug addict might face as they contemplate a life of sobriety. Remember to keep your eyes closed except when choosing another Affirmation Phrase from the menu:

1. Picture one of your more pleasant memories of becoming intoxicated, remember how nice it was and what details made it so pleasantly memorable. Now picture someone, perhaps a friend, who is still enjoying the experience of being intoxicated without a care in the world. Now think about how you are no longer allowed to enjoy that pleasant sense of intoxication or the camaraderie of fellow users, and notice how sad, hurt, disappointed and envious this makes you feel! Now mentally picture yourself as sober, lonely, bored and sad, notice the fear sensations in your stomach, and then apply the AT-T intervention.

2. Think about what a loser you are, a drunk, a sot, a junkie, a hype, an addict—whatever insulting labels you dislike the most when applied to yourself. With your eyes closed, picture yourself as what you consider the worst kind of substance abuser. Does it make you feel embarrassed, ashamed, guilty, disappointed, nervous, hurt and sad? Notice the unpleasant fear-related sensations you feel in your stomach. Then apply the AT-T intervention. You will realize that is not who or what you are anymore.

3. With eyes closed, remember a time when you wished you could stop drinking or using, and then realized that you could not make yourself want to badly enough to actually do it? Does this mental picture make you feel a little sad, worried, guilty, and ashamed, and can you feel the fear-related sensations in your stomach? Now, apply the AT-T intervention. You will realize that is not how you are anymore.

4. Close your eyes and mentally picture what non-drinking or non-using people thought of you as an alcoholic or addict. Keeping your eyes closed, picture yourself as if each and every terrible, ugly thing they thought about you is true, right now. Does this make you feel sad, embarrassed, hurt, ashamed, guilty or nervous? Notice how you feel those fear-related sensations in your stomach. Then, apply the AT-T intervention. You will realize you might have been that way then, but that's not how you are anymore.

5. Close your eyes and imagine yourself in a recovery program, having to surrender to the judgmental know-it-all staff. Notice how this mental picture makes you feel embarrassed, guilty, nervous, annoyed, hostile, impatient and resentful. Picture yourself having to surrender your dignity, like a little boy or a little girl, and notice the fear-type sensations you feel in your stomach. Then apply the AT-T intervention. You will realize you don't really care very much whether they are judging you; they are helping you, and that's all that really matters. You can't imagine yourself guilty or embarrassed.

6. Close your eyes and imagine what that friendly bartender really thought of you as you ordered drink after drink. Keeping your eyes closed, mentally picture yourself as the drunken loser the bartender thought you were. Does this make you feel embarrassed, nervous, guilty or ashamed? Do you feel the fear-related sensations in your stomach by just mentally picturing yourself that way? Now apply the AT-T intervention. You will realize maybe you used to be the person the bartender thought you were, but you aren't that person anymore.

7. With eyes closed, imagine the absolute worst possible outcome if you continue to drink or to use, even if you don't expect anything so horrible will really happen. Mentally picture yourself abandoned by all your friends and family, unemployed, in the gutter, homeless, stupefied, dirty and smelly, sick or in jail. Does this mental picture make you feel scared, worried, anxious, sad or hurt? Notice the fear-related sensations in your stomach. Now, apply the AT-T intervention. You will realize you no longer need to worry about your life turning out like that.

8. Close your eyes and imagine your drinking or drugging buddies don't like you anymore because you have stopped using, you have turned against them, you're no fun anymore. Mentally picture yourself as alone, friendless, maybe feeling a little ashamed because you let them down. Notice that this makes you feel a little sad, hurt, embarrassed, guilty, ashamed, anxious and scared, and notice the fear-related sensations in your stomach. Now apply the AT-T intervention. You will no longer be concerned

about their disapproval of your sobriety.

9. Close your eyes and imagine how dull and empty your life will be when you are sober all the time, how the only people you can hang out with are boring recovered addicts, and the even more boring non-addicts, having to drink ginger ale at parties while others get to drink or use other drugs. Notice how just picturing this makes you feel sad, hurt, disappointed and envious, and notice how you feel fear-related sensations in your stomach. Then, apply the AT-T intervention. You will realize that your life as a non-drinker or non-user isn't boring at all unless you make it that way.

10. Close your eyes and imagine wishing every day for a drink or for some drugs and having to fight the persistent mental picture of how good it would feel to get high. Does this make you feel sad, hurt, nervous, disappointed and worried? Notice the fear-related sensations in your stomach. Then apply the AT-T intervention. You will realize your desire to drink or to use drugs has become much milder, or perhaps is completely gone. You might find you seldom even think about it anymore.

As already pointed out, this is certainly not an exhaustive list of potential fear triggers that might need to be therapeutically addressed by a recovering addict who wants to sustain sobriety without it being a lifelong struggle and without having to make recovery the cornerstone of life. Many addicts will find it surprisingly easy to give up their addiction via AT-T. Others will no doubt have more confidence in the lifelong state of being "in recovery." Individuals who are currently experiencing what they consider success "in recovery" usually reject the very idea that there is such a goal as total recovery, insisting it is the wishful thinking on the part of therapists who have never been addicted and therefore don't really understand what it's like.

To reiterate, Alpha Therapy is not intended to replace AA or The Twelve Steps, or any other recovery program. Added to existing recovery programs, and admittedly as primary treatment in many cases, it is a therapeutic intervention that greatly enhances the individual's chances of maintaining sobriety. In addition, in many cases Alpha Therapy will greatly diminish the need for lifetime dependency on a sophisticated external support system, because the persistent mental cravings that previously plagued the addict or alcoholic will be reduced to a level of occasional images that are easily resisted, or will be gone entirely.

It is arguable that the alcoholic or drug dependent individual is in a sense addicted to the Alpha brain wave-state of consciousness. The increase of Alpha brain waves is associated with a decrease in Beta brain wave dominance. Beta brain waves, attuned to what is seen, heard smelled, tasted, etc., are more dedicated to logical, linear, practical, static, cause and effect, definitive, blaming, labeling, categorizing and judgmental kinds of thinking. Beta brain waves are dominant when the fear and anger emotions are active. Individuals who tend to be less able to induce Alpha brain wave dominance, and who tend to induce excessive Beta brain wave dominance, are more likely to enjoy self-medication via drugs or alcohol that increase Alpha brain wave activity associated with being relaxed and worry free. For most individuals, any temporary increase in Alpha brain wave dominance is peaceful and relaxing.

When alcohol or drugs generate an increase in the production of Alpha brain waves, it usually is experienced as a pleasant respite for those who unknowingly live with almost constant scanning for threats to their self-esteem or social status. This is a high Beta wave activity state of mind. People who are burdened with such a brain wave imbalanced state are usually so used to it they think it's normal. Under more favorable circumstances—such as during meditation or during peak performance in sports or the arts—Alpha brain waves enable some individuals to experience personal or spiritual insights, increased creative thinking, increased depth and breadth of understanding, increased ability to tolerate ambiguity, an overall refreshed view of life, high quality of performance, and so on.

When the increased Alpha brain waves subside and Beta brain waves—the so-called awake state—resume dominance, some of the benefits of expansive thinking can carry over to the awake state in beneficial ways. But this only occurs when the increase in Alpha wave activity occurs naturally, without the use of drugs or alcohol, or when certain drugs are used sacramentally, as with some religious practices, instead of for recreation. Individuals who have used mind-altering substances—peyote, for example—for religious or spiritual purposes in structured, supervised and spiritually goal-directed ceremonies, have experienced risk-free, insightful and lasting spiritual benefits.

Alpha brain waves induced by recreational toxicity occasionally provides some insights, but there are usually no lasting benefits from them. This is because the addict or alcoholic is seeking only respite from chronic threats to self-esteem and social status, and is not anticipating any self-improvement or spiritual benefits. The feeling of respite completely evaporates as the toxicity wears off, and any chance insight loses its impact as sobriety returns with its Beta wave dominance. This explains to a limited extent one of the reasons the drug or alcohol abusing individual looks forward to the next opportunity to return to toxicity.

The significance of changes in brain wave activity associated with alcohol or drug intoxication is easily overlooked. The fact that when intoxicated one becomes vulnerable to some kinds of imprinting is also easily overlooked. Terms like "drug buddies," "drinking buddies," "there's no hope without dope," "getting high," "one more for the road," referring to non-addicts as "lame," etc., represents far more to the recovering client than just casual slang. There is a bonding—imprinting—that occurs when friends become intoxicated together. It involves a degree of blind loyalty somewhat similar to the loyalty one feels to one's parents. It also involves an imprinting of so-called drug values, which include various rationalizations and justifications, as well as some displacement of blame onto the government, the police, the "establishment," parents, unfair expectations in school or on the job and society's double standards. If left untreated, which they usually are, these drug-related imprints remain as hidden obstacles to recovery.

As with any client, the recovering addict, when sober, is still subject to the instinctive need to avoid unpleasant feelings and sensations, even though the preferred avenue is substance abuse. This individual will require the encouragement and direction of the AT-T psychotherapist to identify the fear triggers they have been avoiding by getting high. Fundamentally, their fear triggers are the direct or indirect result of negative paradigms imprinted in childhood, that make them believe that for some unknown reason they are ugly, incompetent and unlovable. Alcohol and drugs provide a temporary escape from concerns about these beliefs.

Simply put, for the client in recovery to have the best possible chance of success, the AT-T psychotherapist needs to guide him or her in identifying and in neutralizing fear triggers in three areas of need. *First*, identify the fear triggers associated with the client's realization that never again will he or she be able to enjoy the guaranteed respite from fear triggers offered by toxic substances. *Second*, identify the fear triggers associated with the bonding and values imprinted while drinking or drugging with fellow users. By remaining sober they are violating some of these imprints. Fortunately, they are not as strong and as inflexible as imprinted paradigms from early childhood. *Third*, identify the fear triggers that resulted from the early childhood imprinting of negative paradigms about being ugly, incompetent and unlovable. These are the fear triggers that made the individual so vulnerable to becoming addicted.

These areas of need can be effectively addressed by Alpha Therapy-Targeting, either alone or in conjunction with an existing program such as AA, The Twelve Steps or with any cognitive program.

Chapter Thirteen
AT-T and Fears, Phobias and Obsessive Compulsive Disorders

ACCORDING TO THE *PSYCHIATRIC DICTIONARY*, *Seventh Edition*, edited by Robert Jean Campbell, M.D., Oxford University Press, 1996, there are three general categories of phobias: Specific Phobias, Social Phobias, and Agoraphobia—fear of open spaces. Agoraphobia is the one for which professional help is the most often sought, and tends to also be the one that most interferes with one's lifestyle. Of the variety of theoretical explanations for phobias the majority seem to be psychoanalytical and tied into presumed sexual aberrations. But this is only a diagnostic theory. No single treatment has stood out as having been effective, though some of them have sometimes helped to alleviate the intensity of fears "caused" by the phobia.

The AT-T psychotherapist addresses the treatment of phobias by directing the client to mentally picture the worst phobic fear scenario they can imagine. Then the client is directed to identify and to mentally picture *the most fear-inducing elements* in the pictured scenario. In other words, the client pictures the worst things about it, and/or the worst things they can imagine happening; i.e., the fear trigger. The client then tells the psychotherapist which of the fear-type emotions they are feeling and the fear-related sensations in their stomach area while just picturing the fear trigger. Then, the psychotherapist guides the client in applying the AT-T intervention to each individual fear trigger.

There might be several fear producing scenarios associated with one phobia. The client mentally pictures each fear-inducing detail individually in each scenario. The AT-T psychotherapist guides the client in applying the AT-T intervention to each one individually. This step-by-step process continues until the phobia no longer exists.

Usually a phobia is produced in some way with imprinted negative paradigms from early childhood. It is rarely necessary to identify how, when and by whom the original paradigm was imprinted. Fortunately, it is usually sufficient to neutralize the phobias—fear triggers—it produced.

It is not unusual for some clients to obsessively visualize aberrant sexual scenarios or other violent scenarios as fear triggers. As with any fear-inducing mental imagery, they are treated with AT-T as fear triggers. A child is not yet sufficiently developed neurologically, so they are extremely vulnerable to being imprinted with negative paradigms—remember, all imprinted paradigms are negative because they tend to be rigid and inflexible. It is easy to understand why they often misinterpret their experiences. It is not surprising that some of their experiences develop into phobias.

Children can very easily acquire, and most of them do, unreasonable beliefs and expectations about themselves and unreasonable beliefs and expectations about how things are or should be and how other people are or should be. Aberrant mental imagery or emerging memories of abuse cannot be automatically assumed by the AT-T psychotherapist to necessarily be an accurate reflection of a client's early childhood experiences. But they can easily be tested for clinically significant fear feelings by the brief application of the AT-T therapeutic intervention.

Negative beliefs and expectations—negative paradigms—usually continue to pose threats to the individual's self-esteem and sense of social status on into adulthood. The list of things, situations and people that have been identified as the object of someone's phobia has increased exponentially. As individuals become more literate and more experienced it is not surprising that their fears can become phobically attached to an increasingly wide variety of objects, situations and people, both real and imaginary.

Fear in one form or another is the underlying theme of phobias. AT-T addresses anything or anyone identified by a client as a fear trigger, whether it is real or imaginary. While a truly frightening experience can produce a kind of phobic reaction to something or to someone—as in post-traumatic stress disorder (PTSD)—it follows that a therapeutic intervention such as AT-T can neutralize it. Further, it can be assumed that vulnerability to a PTSD response results from negative imprinting during early childhood. Once the dynamics of early childhood imprinting and the subsequent fear/anger responses to fear triggers are clearly understood, it becomes rather obvious that imprinted paradigms from early childhood are the root problem. As already explained, the neutralization of fear triggers weakens imprinted paradigms.

Obsessive Compulsive Disorder (OCD):

Research on OCD has focused on neurological dysfunctions in some areas of the brain. Some success is reported through medication to normalize somewhat the functioning of neurotransmitters. This is still the most common form of treatment for OCD. There has also been some development of psychoanalytical theory to explain the disorder, although not so much to cure it. At least a few professionals believe it to be a genetically inherited disorder, due to the presence of OCD in the family history of some OCD clients. While this might be true in some cases, in others it might be like assuming a child who enters the same profession as his father or mother does so for genetic reasons.

Admittedly, AT-T has not yet been tested sufficiently in the treatment of clients accurately diagnosed with OCD. If and when it is used as the primary treatment modality, the approach will not be significantly different from how it is used to neutralize any other psychological—fear-based—problem. Even in cases where OCD is a genetically inherited disorder, it can be assumed that it has generated some self-esteem issues, depending upon the degree to which the client has learned to think of the disorder as inappropriate, odd, shameful or a nuisance, and/or due to the teasing or criticism incurred. In such circumstances Alpha Therapy can alleviate the fear and anger—self-esteem and social status issues—that developed as a result of the disorder.

If operating on the tentative assumption that a given client's OCD is the result of early childhood imprinting, the following are some possible ways for the AT-T psychotherapist to assist a client burdened with OCD.

Obsessive Thought Patterns:

1. Close your eyes and imagine that everyone—or perhaps some significant persons—can read your mind and knows your obsessive thoughts even as you are thinking them. Does this make you feel embarrassed, ashamed, guilty, anxious, nervous, scared, etc.? Keeping your eyes closed, notice where you feel the fear-type sensations in your stomach area. Then, apply the AT-T intervention. You will realize your obsessive thoughts does not make you a lesser person, and that they are just a nuisance.

2. Close your eyes and imagine the person or persons about whom you have hateful, sexual or other inappropriate thoughts is able to read your mind and know your obsessive thoughts even as you are thinking them. Does this make your feel worried, anxious, nervous, embarrassed, scared, ashamed, guilty, panicky,

etc.? Keeping your eyes closed, notice the fear-related sensations in your stomach area. Then, apply the AT-T intervention. You will find you don't worry about that anymore, since they cannot read your mind.

3. Close your eyes and imagine so many people can read your mind that the nature of your obsessive thoughts has gotten around and that everyone thinks you are very, very sick or crazy or disgusting. Keeping your eyes closed, picture yourself as very, very sick or crazy or disgusting. Does this make you feel sad, hurt, disappointed, embarrassed and afraid? Notice the fear-related sensations in your stomach area. Now, apply the AT-T intervention. You will no longer worry about being sick, crazy or disgusting, but just burdened with the nuisance of obsessive thoughts, and you will not worry about what other people think about it.

4. Close your eyes and imagine that having obsessive thought patterns means that there is something really seriously wrong with you, that you are permanently messed up and that you will always have to hide these thoughts from others. Does this make you feel sad, hurt, afraid, disappointed, and worried? Keeping your eyes closed, notice the fear-related sensations you feel in your stomach area. Apply the AT-T therapeutic intervention. You will stop worrying about whether you are "messed up" because you have obsessive thoughts.

Are you getting the idea? Treat *all* your worries as fear triggers, and then use the AT-T intervention to disconnect your fear feelings from each fear trigger you can identify.

Compulsive Behaviors:

Compulsive behaviors often are the result of early childhood dynamics, although some are caused by some as yet unidentified brain dysfunction. Chances are you will never fully understand why you developed compulsive behaviors. But perhaps you've already noticed if you resist acting out your compulsive behavior you become nervous, anxious—fear emotions. This means that resisting the urge to give in to your compulsion is a fear trigger. That is good news! It means you can significantly reduce the problem, or even eliminate it, by using the AT-T intervention.

1. Close your eyes and imagine choosing to hold yourself back from indulging in the compulsive behavior, and notice what kind of fear-type feelings you experience by just thinking about it. Keeping your eyes closed, notice the fear-related sensations in your stomach area. Then, apply the AT-T intervention. It will immediately become easier to resist the compulsion, or the compulsion might be gone entirely.

2. Next, close your eyes again and notice what you are now picturing in your mind; it might be something unpleasant that does not seem obviously related to your compulsive behavior. But trust your own thoughts. Let yourself experience the fear-type feelings caused by that mental picture, and notice the fear-related sensations in your stomach area. Then apply the AT-T intervention. You will notice that mental picture is no longer a fearful one.

3. It can be surprising sometimes where this line of mental imagery may lead. Don't panic; go with the mental pictures. Don't let your fears prevent you from recognizing the fear triggers. Yes, it happens. It isn't fun to admit fear triggers to yourself or to a psychotherapist. Just remember that you have the ability to permanently disconnect your fear feelings from those triggers. Write them down if they sometimes come into your mind at odd times. When you have an opportunity, you can apply the AT-T intervention to every one of them.

Due to the complex dynamics that are sometimes involved in the above disorders, it is recommended that an experienced AT-T psychotherapist guide the client through treatment.

Chapter Fourteen
The Importance of Cognitive Therapy

ALPHA THERAPY-TARGETING (AT-T) DOES NOT directly address social skills, problem solving skills, analytical skills and decision-making skills, although when fear triggers are neutralized, some of these skills do show spontaneous improvement. Primarily it addresses thinking errors such as keeping score, poor me, helplessness, justifying, selfishness, minimizing, and victim stance via the alleviation of fear triggers that seem to have made thinking errors spontaneous and seemingly necessary. After addressing a number of key fear triggers, the mindless fear and anger response of the Fight-or-Flight (F-or-F) instinct begin to appear primitive and counterproductive and the client feels more self-confident experiencing the real world and the daily ups and downs of life as they really are.

The client becomes able to perceive a wider array of options in these areas instead of experiencing the tunnel vision, blaming, denial, insensitivity to others, and so on, generated by the F-or-F emotions. They begin to rely more on knowledge, understanding, insight, tolerance, patience, social and communication skills, problem solving skills and positive leadership skills and all the other resources of a more humanized person. The exception would be the individual reared in a poorly socialized or a criminogenic family environment.

Realistically, no individuals—especially young people—possess all the necessary information and skills needed to enable them to always make the best decisions, to always get their needs met in the most skillful or effective manner, or to always perform optimally in every situation. But there is a large minority of both adults and minors, individuals who are deficient, some quite severely, in such knowledge and skills. Most juveniles committed to correctional institutions for rehabilitative treatment due to delinquency are notably deficient in cognitive skills and problem-solving skills and are habituated to the use of a wide variety of thinking errors and distorted values.

AT-T can eliminate the F-or-F emotional reactions that interfere with intellectual functioning, and this can render the juvenile more receptive to learning better thinking skills and knowledge which are at the heart of Cognitive Therapies. AT-T will not in and of itself compensate for deficiencies and distorted values that have accrued from being reared in an asocial or antisocial environment. Most troubled youths, and many adults as well, still require some form of Cognitive Therapy.

Young people in particular will need professional help to enable them to recognize and to neutralize the fear triggers that interfere with their ability to learn what they need from cognitive programs. Troubled young people tend to occasionally test helping professionals, to observe whether they have been "practicing what they have been preaching." Most staff in the helping professions are suffering from the same fear trigger problems as are the troubled youths, though obviously not to such a degree as to have made them vulnerable to criminogenic peer influence. The staff members should have the right to receive the same AT-T treatment services that should also be provided for the youths in correctional facilities, drug treatment facilities and residential treatment programs.

It has been said that without language we would be unable to think. It is generally accepted that thinking involves words, pictures and emotions. So it seems to follow that the more limited one's ability to mentally combine words, pictures and emotions in meaningful, pro-social ways, the more limited is one's ability to think, to communicate and to act in meaningful pro-social ways. In fact, to many delinquent youths pro-social thinking is incomprehensible and pointless!

Adolescents and adults who display a pattern of poor decision-making are in critical need of more pro-social words, more pro-social pictures and fewer fear triggers that require chronic defensive scanning. This is demonstrated in the way both juvenile and adult delinquents often struggle to grasp logical reasoning and principles of cause and effect that impact on their daily lives. It is also demonstrated in their relative inability to recognize the self-defeating, counterproductive and often absurd values and behaviors of their delinquent peers.

Many adolescents have never developed an interest in exercising pro-social evaluative thinking because it has not occurred to them that such thinking has any particular value, and in their early childhood they have never seen anyone engaging in it. Both adolescents and many adults tend to "find each other" and to form social subgroups. This can have the effect of locking in their limited cognitive abilities and their distorted values, especially if drugs are involved. In such cases, a comprehensive Cognitive Therapy program is necessary, working interactively with AT-T—and/or EMDR, if it is made available.

Adolescents and adults who are involved with gangs, drugs, and criminality tend to be severely deficient in pro-social vocabulary, pro-social communication skills and positive social concepts, as well as in the positive mental pictures that are fundamental for higher level thinking. Cognitive Therapy alone, even that which addresses comprehensively the words and pictures of pro-social thinking, is not very successful because it does not diminish the various forms of fear and anger that reinforce criminal values and seem to perpetuate reliance on thinking errors.

We evaluate most symptoms in terms of whether they are clinically significant. We look at their severity or intensity, their frequency, whether they interfere significantly with the client's job performance, relationships, morale, self-esteem, decision-making, personal safety, the safety of others or threat to the community, and so on. Some symptoms cry out for intervention. Other symptoms can be tolerated or managed sufficiently by the client and do not necessarily require intervention.

This is realistic since the science of psychotherapy is not at a point where all negative symptoms can be reduced to zero. In fact, we cannot always accurately identify what is a symptom and what is not, nor can we yet accurately define what is optimally normal or healthy. Theoretically the ideal is the complete elimination of the function of the F-or-F instinctive emotional response, but currently that is just a theory. However, within the range of symptoms that are obviously counterproductive, self-limiting, that interfere with self-esteem, are destructive of relationships, or harmful to others, there are endless opportunities for AT-T psychotherapists to contribute in a meaningful way to the quality of a client's life.

A healthy trust of the psychotherapist usually develops after a client has experienced clear and lasting benefits from AT-T sessions. Until such time, a client's trust, if any, of the psychotherapist is necessarily based upon wishful thinking and it has little basis in experiential reality. Alpha Therapy provides the psychotherapist with the unusual opportunity of being able to demonstrate, perhaps from the very first session, that the benefits of AT-T are real, desirable and lasting! This in itself is very unusual in the entire field of psychotherapy, with the possible exception of EMDR—because it is so similar to AT-T.

This is of utmost importance, because once the client has realized some clear and lasting benefits from the AT-T intervention, the AT-T psychotherapist begins to have increased credibility. Delinquent clients become increasingly willing to listen to advice offered by the therapist. The client becomes increasingly receptive to how the Alpha Therapist interprets events, emotional states, values and thought processes in the client's life.

It is obviously of critical importance that the AT-T psychotherapist be a reasonably well-balanced person, and have considerable personal experience with the application of AT-T to their own self-esteem and social status fear triggers. He or she needs to be free of rigid concepts of right and wrong, except in cases where a client presents an obvious physical threat to themselves or to others. In addition, the longer term client needs to periodically Target the Alpha psychotherapist. This serves two purposes. *First*, it reduces the likelihood of the client becoming too emotionally dependent on the Alpha Therapist. *Second*, when entering into the discussion of a new area of a client's fear triggers, the client often becomes evasive because it means fresh disclosures of fear-type feelings and/or beliefs that such disclosures display weakness, incompetence or ugliness.

The client's perception of the psychotherapist as "all wise and all knowing," is to some degree necessary and to some degree unavoidable anyway. After all, the AT-T psychotherapist is actually guiding the client in the dismantling of his or her fear triggers. This, to a delinquent, is a big deal! At first it can seem almost magical, it is so unexpected. But knowing how simple a matter it is to do away with a fear trigger via the AT-T intervention makes it only a little bit easier for a delinquent client to bring their remaining fear triggers to conscious awareness and then to disclose them to the AT-T psychotherapist.

On the other hand, the client has the right to say, "That's enough. I'm satisfied with the progress I've made. I want to stop working on my fear triggers now." If the client is not still burdened with needs or impulses that will likely be harmful to themselves or to others, or get them arrested again, then the AT-T psychotherapist needs to let go, even when it is clear that much more could be accomplished on the client's behalf.

Chapter Fifteen
How to Assess the Outcome of an AT-T Intervention

AGAIN, DO NOT EXPECT A WOW! response or a display of intense relief from a client upon the successful resolution of a fear trigger. It doesn't work like that. If anything, you will see a look of slightly embarrassed bewilderment, and perhaps a look of confusion. They can't understand how it is that their immediate mental picture of what was a "fear trigger" is no longer a fear trigger. In fact, it's as if they can't quite understand why they thought it was such a threat in the first place!

In over 25 years of specializing in the Alpha Therapy-Targeting (AT-T) intervention with male and female adults, teenagers and children—and with my own fear triggers—I have had only one 17-year-old delinquent say, "Oh, I feel so relieved!" When he said that I knew immediately that he had only pretended to silently repeat the Affirmation Phrases in his mind with his eyes closed. When I later confronted him about it he laughed, seeming pleased I had recognized his dishonesty. This occurred in a juvenile corrections setting with an active gang member.

To obtain an accurate assessment of the outcome, get the client's mind off the fear trigger on which you have just completed an apparently successful AT-T intervention. Engage him or her in the search for another fear trigger, or perhaps engage the client in a conversation about some unrelated topic. You can even wait a day or two, or longer, if you wish. Don't wait too long, though, because the client might have trouble remembering that it ever was a fear trigger! Discuss with the client some fear triggers that have already been addressed with the AT-T intervention. Notice the facial expression, the affect, changes in verbal expression used to talk about it, whether it is pictured differently, or if it can be pictured at all.

On the other hand, I have worked with a few delinquent male adolescents who have a few weeks later informed me that their original goal had been to prove to me that AT-T would not work for them. But these youths had actually participated correctly in the AT-T process, and the benefits had accrued in spite of their negative intent.

Here is a list of some possible outcomes that would indicate success in disconnecting a client's fear-type responses to a fear trigger:

1. The client cannot sustain a mental picture of the person or the personal flaw or the situation that constituted the fear trigger for more than a few seconds at a time. *This means the fear trigger is no longer "emotionally loaded" so the mental picture of it can no longer sustain the client's interest.*
2. The client can picture the person or the personal flaw, or the situation that constituted the fear trigger for a little while, but it seems benign and harmless now. *The client's fear reactions were the reason it had been perceived as a significant fear trigger.*
3. The client can only picture the person or the personal flaw or the situation in a friendly or ordinary manner. *Now that the fear reaction is disconnected, the one-time fear trigger is now perceived by the client as just an ordinary, non-threatening experience.*

4. The client can still picture the person or the personal flaw or the situation, but it now seems trivial and hardly worth discussing. *The fear trigger's only importance to the client was due to its potential for inducing a fear-type emotional reaction.*

5. The client can still picture the person, personal flaw or the situation, but in a more understanding, forgiving context. *Since the fear trigger is no longer perceived by the client as a personal threat, it can now be viewed in a compassionate context.*

The AT-T psychotherapist will occasionally encounter an interesting variation in outcome to an intervention. The client's fear feelings will seem to be in layers. The first application of AT-T to a particular fear trigger might eliminate just one of the fear feelings the client had reported experiencing. Re-Targeting the same fear trigger will eliminate another fear feeling previously reported by the client. By Targeting the same fear trigger for a third time, the final fear-type feeling is gone. Three layers of feelings, disconnected one at a time, is the most I have observed in over 25 years of specializing in the AT-T therapeutic interventions with hundreds of clients. It seems to occur only rarely. Usually just one application of the AT-T intervention is sufficient to disconnect all the various forms of fear associated with a single fear trigger.

You might want to maintain some simple form of record of which fear triggers have been treated with the AT-T intervention, because your clients will tend to forget most of their fear triggers ever existed after a few months. It is not known at this time why there is an almost universal tendency for them to forget their fear triggers ever existed, once they have been neutralized.

It is rarely necessary for the therapist to reframe a troubling dilemma for a client, once the associated fear triggers have been resolved via AT-T. The usual result is that clients tend to spontaneously do their own more positive and healthy reframing of the situation without needing the therapist's assistance.

To the Reader, the Client and the Therapist
Some Good Reasons to "Face Your Fears" via AT-T:

1. You'll begin to realize it's not necessary to do all the things you were afraid to do. Now you choose not to do some of them for non-fear-based reasons.

2. Targeting your fears now means your choices are becoming more rational and less emotion-based.

3. Fear and anger interfere with your functional intelligence; as you Target your fears it's like becoming more intelligent.

4. Every time you Target a fear trigger, your self-esteem increases in most all areas.

5. Your anger and fear feelings are like a road map directing you to increasing your self-esteem, your self-confidence and your functional intelligence.

6. Start Targeting the fear triggers that make you feel resentful or angry, and pretty soon you'll notice you don't get mad very often.

7. Eventually you'll notice that when you do get mad, it doesn't last very long; and, it more like just getting a little annoyed.

8. Eventually you'll notice that you are thinking more creatively—in a practical way as well as in a spiritual way.

9. Eventually you'll notice that you don't worry very much about things any more; but you do pay attention and you deal with difficult situations more effectively.

10. Eventually you'll notice you seldom think about whether or not you are accepted by peers, except that however much you are accepted will be enough.

11. Eventually you'll notice that you seldom think about whether you are rejected by peers; and, when you are rejected—and everybody is rejected from time to time—it won't matter to you very much, if you notice it at all.

12. You don't have to be excellent at everything you do; and it's okay when you're not sure what to do next.

When you "face your fears" by Targeting your fear triggers, you're getting rid of a lot of the emotional "junk" that was interfering with your intelligence, your self-esteem and your self-confidence, even when you weren't thinking about your fear triggers. You are on your way to becoming "all you can be." Most people don't know what they can accomplish in life; they never find that out. They spend a lot of energy trying to appear more self-confident than they really feel. They hope other people won't notice how afraid they are. In fact, most people don't want to know about their own fears. This is because they don't believe there's anything they can do about them, except pretend most of them don't exist, or get mad as hell to cover them up.

Chapter Sixteen
Things That Can Interfere with the AT-T Intervention

AS WITH ALL SUCH METHODOLOGIES, ALPHA Therapy-Targeting (AT-T) is neither foolproof nor is it a cure-all. For instance, it does not take the place of cognitive training, when there is a clinically significant need for increased or improved social skills, problem solving skills and thinking and reasoning skills.

As has been previously stated ad infinitum, the unique contribution of AT-T is that it quickly and permanently neutralizes fear triggers in any form, whether trivial or severe, real or imaginary, in the past, present or in the imagined future. Further, it points out clearly that anger is a defense mechanism, activated by some form of fear trigger, or by the anticipation of a fear trigger. With that reiterated, it is important to point out what kinds of things or situations can interfere with the successful outcome of an AT-T intervention.

First, the client must be able to set aside their anger feelings and accept the fact that one or more fear-type feelings were the immediate cause of their anger defense mechanism. Then they must be willing and able to identify the parts of the experience that were the most fear provoking. Obviously, few people can set aside feelings of anger when the perceived cause of them has just recently occurred. So a new client might need time to allow their anger to subside a little, since it is nearly impossible to set aside intense anger.

The exception to the above paragraph is that person who has used AT-T successfully enough times to be clearly aware that fear-type feelings always precede the anger defense mechanism. Individuals who have already done considerable anger work with AT-T often need only be reminded—or to remind themselves—of that fact. It is sometimes surprising how quickly they are able to set their anger aside and get in touch with the underlying fear feelings.

Second, occasionally, though not often, the AT-T psychotherapist encounters a client who exhibits affect and behavior that is generally referred to as "hyper." An individual who seems chronically hyper likely has difficulty generating sufficient Alpha brain waves when they are needed. To my knowledge this particular disorder has not been researched adequately, except within the context of AD/HD, bipolar disorder and a few other disorders. Therefore, I am extrapolating on research results not directly related to people whose only problem is being chronically hyper.

Individuals who tend to be hyper have difficulty paying sustained attention, a critical requirement in cognitive treatment programs. An individual might be in severe need of cognitive treatment, but they likely are producing too much Beta brain wave activity, causing them to be distracted by other people in the group, as well as by their own errant thoughts. The mental aspect of excessive Beta brain wave activity and frequent mental distraction are very difficult to notice unless the psychotherapist knows what to look for, and even more importantly, understands the significance of this type of inattention.

Individuals who are correctly diagnosed with AD/HD can be

expected to produce Beta brain waves and Alpha brain waves erratically and at inappropriate times. Most clients with AD/HD are unpredictable in this regard. But, sometimes they seem to welcome the encouragement of a trusted psychotherapist to produce Alpha brain waves at the strategic time. Of course brain waves, per se, are seldom mentioned to a client. But the repetitions of the Affirmation Phrases, the repetitious eye movement of EMDR, or whatever is repetitiously done, is for the purpose of generating a brief increase in the production of Alpha brain waves.

Trust is important because individuals with AD/HD, as well as clients with other disorders that have caused them to incur excessive criticism, will find it difficult initially to trust the psychotherapist. They will expect to do poorly in therapy, as they have in so many other things. Many people have experienced a lifetime of being criticized for not paying attention, for daydreaming, for being too active, for being insensitive to others' feelings, for not studying enough in school, for not learning fast enough and for not understanding quickly enough.

In addition, there are many reasons for being hyper besides AD/HD. There are numerous people who have brain dysfunctions who would not have been diagnosed by a regular physician. Many children, especially males, have experienced fairly severe head bumps while playing in sports, play fighting, with friends, or just by accident. Mild concussions are fairly common, and there is usually no medical treatment beyond the recommendation to take it easy for a while and to get some extra rest. But a head bump that is not considered especially severe at the time can produce damage to the brain, because the brain has been banged against the inside of the skull. Probably most males are at least slightly brain damaged because of such experiences while growing up.

The damage to the brain and to the healthy interaction of all the brain waves and brain centers can last a lifetime. It can go unnoticed if there are no symptoms significant enough to bring up the question of possible brain damage. It might even be considered of little importance if the individual's work and/or lifestyle doesn't happen to make any significant demands on the use of the part of the brain that has been rendered dysfunctional. As brain mapping comes into more common use there will probably be many an applicant who will not be accepted for sensitive employment; i.e., airline pilots, military pilot training, etc. The mere fact of brain damage will not be the issue in such cases. The issue will be whether there is significant dysfunction in the areas of the brain considered critical to optimal performance on the job or in the job training itself.

Interestingly, the brain has a rather remarkable potential for redundancy. It is known that the brain sloughs off unused neural pathways periodically by the thousands, particularly during the first fifteen years of life. But there are innumerable unused neural pathways that can be used to compensate for much that might have been lost due to brain damage. Sometimes this occurs naturally and sometimes it requires training. Material lost via brain damage can sometimes be simply relearned, with the individual remaining unaware that new neural pathways are being formed for that purpose. Neurofeedback Therapists are demonstrating that brain waves can be retrained through practice with Neurofeedback equipment programmed specifically for the individual where it is most needed.

I have found no research yet on brain wave training to specifically alleviate hyperactivity. But extrapolating on research of brain dysfunctions that include hyperactivity, is seems likely that practice with an inexpensive hand-held Biofeedback instrument would enable a person to train their brain to generate increased Alpha brain wave activity when needed. From reviewing the research of related brain wave diagnosis and training it appears that practice on the hand-held Biofeedback instrument for about twenty minutes a day, four or five days a week, for three or four weeks could significantly decrease a client's tendency to be hyper and at the same time increase their ability to normally produce Alpha brain waves when they are need for a given situation.

Third, when working with delinquent males there is the added element of a possible oppositional and defiant disorder. This can result in attempts by the delinquent client to find ways to delay or redirect the AT-T intervention process. This can be in the form of excessive talking, attempts to engage the AT-T psychotherapist in conversation about tangential topics, or, even arguing about what the client thinks are the shortcomings of the AT-T intervention. In more extreme cases of O&DD the client might only pretend to participate in the intervention. Thus, they attempt to prove to the psychotherapist that the AT-T intervention is worthless. This can be another reason why it is a good idea to assess the outcome of the intervention by engaging the client later on in talking about a fear trigger that has been previously addressed by the AT-T intervention. As with any client, observe for changes in verbal expression, tone of voice, indications of blaming or justifying, facial expressions and other body movements that can indicate whether the fear trigger has been neutralized.

Fourth, most psychotherapists have not been addressing the emotions that bring on and reinforce a delinquent client's troublesome behaviors. The only exception is the insistence of those who believe cognitive therapy is adequate for addressing emotions. They continue to believe in cognitive therapy even though it is not "evidence based"; i.e., no cognitive therapy program has achieved more than a 25-30% success rate. Aside from these poor success rates, the wide use of cognitive therapies has clearly demonstrated that "talk therapy" has little lasting effect when it comes to the negative emotions that reinforce delinquent behavior.

Many delinquent clients have learned in other cognitive treatment programs to say what they have observed the psychotherapists want to hear. After guiding delinquent clients in the AT-T intervention hundreds of times, the AT-T psychotherapist gradually begins to pay more attention to a client's facial expressions, body movements, verbal expression, tone of voice, the presence or absence of blaming or justifying, and so on. After guiding hundreds of delinquent male youths in thousands of AT-T interventions, some rules of thumb have emerged. Of course, a psychotherapist must be alert to exceptions to any rule of thumb. One rule of thumb is to expect any client to report fear-type sensations in the upper, middle or lower stomach, in the throat, or—when Targeting a fear trigger that brought on extreme embarrassment—in the face.

Fifth, if a delinquent client reports feeling fear-type feelings in their head, in their shoulders, in their back, in their arms or hands, and especially in the chest area, you should remind him or her to set aside their anger and to concentrate only on fear feelings. The problem here is that the anger defense mechanism is contaminating the AT-T intervention by preventing the youth from feeling their fear feelings. If this is the problem, little value will come out of the intervention. Remind them to think in terms of "poor me." Fear-type feelings are, after all, victim feelings.

Sixth, sometimes when a client tries to mentally visualize a fear trigger situation, it's like entering a maze. They have trouble deciding on which fear trigger to focus. They are experiencing a complexity of many interrelated fear triggers. While it's a good thing that they can so easily think of fear triggers, it is very difficult for them to work on them one at a time. Usually there is no key fear trigger; rather, there are many triggers. This is because self-esteem fears and social fears can appear in many different scenarios and situations. There are also often a number of individuals who played a part in a client's early childhood negative imprinting.

This does not present a problem for AT-T. It simply means the psychotherapist will have to use stronger directive guidance to assist the client in making choices regarding which fear triggers to work on and in what order. Fortunately, it is not usually necessary to apply the AT-T intervention to every fear trigger in this client's emotional maze. As previously mentioned, some fear triggers will be neutralized without being therapeutically addressed, simply because of their close similarity to another fear trigger that has been addressed via AT-T. And remember, it makes no difference whether the client's memory of events is accurate. AT-T is not seeking the truth; it is seeking fear triggers, whether real or imaginary, so that they can be neutralized.

As the client becomes increasingly able to recognize the many fear triggers that occur almost from moment to moment on a daily basis, he or she might begin to think the AT-T treatment might go on forever. Fortunately, this is not the case. Fear triggers exist in what might be called subgroups. To oversimplify, imagine a table. You cut off one leg and it still stands; it can still function as a table. When you cut off a second leg the table falls. It is no longer a functional table. Whenever a client neutralizes a fear trigger it weakens the subgroup of fear triggers that are similar. After a client neutralizes several fear triggers of a subgroup, the whole subgroup of similar fear triggers is neutralized along with them. Many fear triggers will be neutralized before the client even becomes aware of their existence.

Another way to describe this phenomenon: Some clients have elected to start making a list of the many fear triggers they recognize throughout the day. They self-apply the AT-T intervention on several of them every evening just before bedtime. But the list keeps getting longer and longer. After a few weeks, though, they notice that some of the fear triggers on the list that they have not yet worked on are no longer fear triggers—for the reasons just explained in the previous paragraph. Their list begins to shrink. After several weeks I have had a delinquent youth ask me if it's okay that they didn't notice any fear triggers all weekend! They are so used to adding fear triggers to their list they are in wonderment when for a few days there was nothing to add!

Usually a client will have little or no resistance to disclosing to the AT-T psychotherapist what fear trigger they are visualizing. But occasionally a client will feel hesitant because it might make them sound disrespectful toward one of their parents, or because they think it is so ugly that they fear the psychotherapist will disapprove of them. This fear of disclosure can be discomforting to psychotherapists who are used to cognitive therapy and always knowing—or so they think—the content of the therapy process. This is much less the case with an AT-T psychotherapist. Get used to it; remember that your purpose is to assist the client in neutralizing fear triggers, with only brief indulgences in occasional bits of talk therapy when and if it seems helpful to the client. After the "secret" fear trigger has been Targeted the client will likely be quite willing to disclose what it was.

Needless to say, the cooperation of clients is essential to the conducting of individual or group AT-T sessions. Clients just starting out will think it is very strange to be identifying and disclosing their fear triggers, something they have been trying to think about as little as possible except to keep hidden from view. Verbal encouragement can help, at least for the duration of an AT-T therapy session. If the AT-T psychotherapist can share some personal examples of how they have applied the intervention to neutralize some of their own self-esteem and social status fear triggers, this will instill some additional trust in the psychotherapist and in the AT-T intervention. It is definitely a trust issue, since clients are expected to become conscious of what and who they are afraid of and to disclose it to someone else. It is never a pleasant experience for the client, but after a fear trigger is neutralized they often can barely remember how difficult it was to mentally picture it and to describe it.

Seventh, quite a few clients will enthusiastically express the intention of doing some self-applied AT-T interventions. Be cautious in such cases. Some will follow through admirably with this intention. What we blithely refer to as human nature, though, is actually more animal than human. Animals react to the "avoid pain, seek pleasure" principle very crudely and directly; but so do most humans. As a client becomes more humanized via the AT-T intervention he or she begins to understand that *"pain is fear and pleasure is being truly fearless."* When some clients say, "Hey, I can do this by myself, can't I?" what they often mean is, "I don't want to do this anymore." Since it is usually rather unpleasant to mentally picture a fear trigger, many clients will keep putting it off, and sometimes never get around to doing it. This is something the

AT-T psychotherapist needs to watch for. In many cases the AT-T treatment must be done in individual or group sessions or it won't ever get done at all. Recognize this as fairly typical human avoidance behavior and settle for doing as much for the client as possible as long as he or she will keep participating in sessions.

Particularly in such cases, it is recommended that AT-T psychotherapists direct the client into identifying and mentally picturing what appears to be the most important fear triggers, those that seem to be interfering the most negatively in their lives. As soon as it appears feasible, guide the client into those more sensitive areas.

Chapter Seventeen
Generic Guide to Self-Esteem Fears

EVERYONE HAS SOME SELF-ESTEEM FEARS. NO one is lucky enough to not have any. In the first place, there are no perfect parents, so all parents make mistakes. In the second place, no one knows how to rear a child in a socialized manner without interfering to some extent with their self-esteem, whether uncaringly or unknowingly. Extended family members and family friends also commonly interfere with a child's self-esteem, also either uncaringly or unknowingly. It appears nobody gets a "free ride" through life. During the first decade of a person's life it is simply too easy to imprint negative paradigms.

Imprinted negative paradigms—all are negative, not always because of their content, but because of their inflexibility—are defined as unrealistic, unfulfillable beliefs and expectations about the world, about other people and about one's self. Even so-called "good" paradigms, such as respect for parents, religious and spiritual beliefs, altruism, work ethics, and so on, are considered negative by those who use AT-T because of their inflexibility. They interfere with one's learning, and with one's personal change, growth and development. These paradigms are what generate fear triggers in later life. Fear triggers are threats of violation of the dictates of one's paradigms. It is not necessary to identify the original paradigms or who imprinted them. Neutralizing the fear triggers they cause is sufficient to weaken them.

People worry about being too fat, too thin, too tall, too short, to light skinned, too dark skinned, being too big, too small. They worry that they are ugly or at least unattractive, dumb, boring, failures, losers, unlovable, not likable, and on and on. Such worries interfere with one's self-esteem, sense of social status, and therefore self-confidence. Fear triggers also lower one's functional intelligence—even when one is not currently thinking about them!

What do you worry about? Do you sometimes hesitate to reach out to other people or to opportunities? Of course you do! Most everyone does. Use this opportunity to identify and list your worries—fear triggers—and discover how easily and quickly you can disconnect those fear triggers, permanently! Liberate your natural sense of self-esteem, your natural intelligence and the self-confidence it provides.

Take another look at Packets #2, #6 and #7 in Chapter Six for guidance in identifying your fear triggers in various areas of self-esteem and sense of social status.

Some Important Points:

Insults, disrespectful comments, putdowns and mean-spirited teasing only hurt your feelings or embarrass you if you already have even the slightest secret worry—fear trigger—that in some perhaps indefinable way they might be true! For example, if you feel a little hurt inside because someone called you a jerk, it's because in some secret but unclear way you have always worried that you are, or might be, a jerk—whatever the term jerk means to you, since the term cannot be clearly defined.

Most everyone has such worries, until they neutralize them by using the AT-T intervention. Most everyone worries that they don't quite measure up, but they don't know exactly how they don't measure up! So, close your eyes and picture that indefinable fear trigger any way you can, notice the kinds of fears you feel while just picturing it, notice the fear-related sensations in your stomach area. Then apply the AT-T intervention. Your concerns about that indefinable personal flaw or shortcoming will have disappeared forever.

There is no monster in the basement just because the light bulb down there is burnt out! Yet, how does your stomach feel when you have to go down there to change the bulb, especially if it's dark and stormy outside and you've been watching a scary movie on TV? The fear trigger might not be real, but your fear and nervousness are quite real. Close your eyes and mentally picture the worst thing you can imagine waiting for you down there in that dark basement, and note the various fear feeling and the fear-related sensations in your stomach area. Then apply the AT-T intervention. That kind of situation will never again be a fear trigger for you, ever!

Oddly enough, your fear triggers, even the little ones, are your stepping stones to becoming truly humanized. Continue to identify your fear triggers, and continue using the AT-T intervention to disconnect or neutralize them, one by one, and you will gradually stop living your life according to the dictates of your negative paradigms. Your judgments, opinions, decisions and actions will no longer be guided by your fear and anger, however slight they might be. Animals don't have this choice, but you do!

You will become calmer, more self-confident, you will begin to think more clearly in all kinds of situations, and you will begin to have the full use of your natural intelligence. You will no longer have to depend on your *anger defense mechanism*, or be *constantly scanning for potential fear triggers* in order to feel safe.

Chapter Eighteen
AT-T and Juvenile Offenders

Self-Esteem

ALPHA THERAPY-TARGETING (AT-T) SPECIFICALLY neutralizes fear triggers. A fear trigger, once neutralized via AT-T, will never again be a fear trigger in that individual's lifetime. Fear tends to magnify whatever is perceived by an individual as the "cause" of that fear. For this reason AT-T should perhaps be the intervention of choice for addressing the fears that undermine self-esteem and intensify the need for peer approval.

We know that fears of personal insufficiency, fears of not quite measuring up, fears of peer disapproval, and so on, are symptomatic of low self-esteem. This is extremely important when it comes to the rehabilitation of offenders, especially teenage offenders. As important as this is—it has been known for decades!—it is seldom addressed effectively in treatment centers or juvenile corrections treatment programs, except for diagnostic purposes.

Those who have confidence in treatment programs that rely primarily on cognitive therapies—misplaced confidence, as evidenced by the 70-75% failure rates—will often insist they are adequately addressing the emotions that cause and reinforce delinquency. They usually attribute the 70-75% failure rate to "client resistance," or they blame it on the failure of other staff to follow through properly with their roles in whatever cognitive therapy is being used. In fact, some of the meager success rate is more due to the onset of maturity, as well as the desire to avoid adult imprisonment.

The teenager seeks peer companionship as part of his or her gradual transition into a sense of young adulthood and the associated sense of independence. The seeking of peer approval and companionship seems to be a part of the developmental stage of transition that begins to occur at about age eleven or twelve. This is sometimes referred to as "individualizing away from the family." It does not mean the eleven- or twelve-year-old child wants to be completely independent. But she or he does want to have some trial adventures outside the family's protective sphere of influence.

As a true beginner in the adventure of finding out what it might feel like to be a young adult, the child makes mistakes. This is why they tend to find comfort and security by bonding to a peer group, if one is available. Partly because they have perceived adults as seeming relatively calm and confident, teenagers attempt to appear self-confident and sure of themselves—fearless. They and their friends know it's an act, adults who observe them can usually tell it's an act. But since children rarely hear adults talk about having self-esteem fears or social status fears, therefore teenagers seldom talk with each other—or with their parents— about their self-esteem and social status fears either.

In general, anyone or anything that seems to interfere with the ease of this transition into young adulthood is perceived by the child as a threat to their self-esteem and/or social status. A teenager fears the prospect of not having at least one close friend outside the family. The transition into young adulthood can be frightening to a teenager who feels friendless.

After years of practicing denial, justification, blaming and various other thinking errors—learned in early childhood by observing adults—no teenager likes to remind themselves, let alone disclose to a psychotherapist, how much of their personal integrity they have compromised—and still do—to avoid the risk of peer disapproval, embarrassment or of being friendless. This applies particularly to teenagers who have been repeatedly delinquent and have finally been sent by the juvenile court to a correctional institution.

It is the psychotherapist's job to assist the delinquent teenager in overcoming this natural reluctance by providing the reassurance necessary for them to believe it is truly safe to disclose their fears in a therapy session. Some teenage delinquents will have especially strong resistance to such disclosures, likely due to distorted and/or antisocial family values.

Test it Yourself First

Alpha Therapy-Targeting is deceptively simple. It can seem like New Age nonsense until the parent, the coach, the teacher, the clinician—or the reader—tests it by applying it to themselves first. You have likely avoided public speaking, avoided applying for a particular job or for a promotion, avoided certain people who seem intimidating, and you likely wish there were some differences in your body configuration.

No matter how intriguing AT-T might seem, you will hesitate to put it to use with your children, your athletes, your music students, or your clients, or with teenage delinquents, unless you have proved to your personal satisfaction that AT-T does what this book says it will do. If you have doubts about whether it works, your doubts will communicate to the person you are trying to help. This will cause them to have difficulty following your directions. You will gradually begin using what is more familiar and more comfortable—cognitive therapy: the "therapeutic" lecture.

Starting Out

When starting AT-T a teenage delinquent will have no idea what benefits to expect. In fact, because the AT-T intervention is so simple a teenager will no doubt think it's kind of silly and will not expect any benefit at all—much like yourself, until you've tested it on your own self-esteem fears and social status fears. Teenagers, especially teenage delinquents, can harbor a distrust of authority figures, especially counselors and psychotherapists. Take the time to explain some principles of AT-T, such as the anger defense mechanism, what constitutes a fear trigger, and some of your own before-and-after experiences.

Each psychotherapist will have their own way of starting out, whether with a group or with one individual. A "most scary memory" can be a good start because it will probably be easy for the teenager to identify what made it so scary. My "most embarrassing experience" can be a good start for the same reason. Such fear triggers, also called Targets, will likely be easily disclosed by teenagers. The ways of starting out with AT-T are limitless. In a way it really doesn't matter very much, because it's the outcome that's important. How aggressively you start out in a group setting will depend on the constituency of the group as well as your own style.

Emphasize that there is no thrill or wow! reaction when a fear trigger is neutralized. There have been clients who didn't notice the change until it was mentioned—often by someone other than the psychotherapist! Chapter Fourteen describes how to evaluate the outcome of an AT-T intervention. Once a teenage delinquent has experienced several successful outcomes, he or she will become more enthusiastic and trusting of both the psychotherapist and the AT-T intervention.

By introducing the Packets—see Chapter Six—the psychotherapist gradually moves the teenage delinquent toward remembering and disclosing increasingly important fear triggers, the ones that have played a more crucial part in his or her decision to seek the approval and companionship of other delinquents. Gradually the teenage delinquent begins to feel it's okay—emotionally safe—to disclose more sensitive fear triggers. Because of the fear of losing peer approval the teenager will have repeatedly violated his or her own ethical standards. For peer approval the teenage delinquent will have even risked the sense of still having a place in their family.

The psychotherapist explains to the teenage delinquent that there are no perfect parents, and that all parents make mistakes. Hopefully the teenager begins to feel it is emotionally safe to disclose hurtful things said or done to them by their parents, mistakes that had the unintended—or sometimes intended—effect of imprinting excessive fear or excessive shame, which in turn had the effect of undermining their self-esteem, their sense of social status and their self-confidence.

Anger

Human anger, as that of most animals, is primarily a defense mechanism. The anger defense mechanism in animals is sometimes due to fears of invasion of their territory, interference with their immediate food supply, endangerment of their young, threat of physical attack, competition for mating opportunities, and so on. But with humans it is usually threats of embarrassment, loss of peer approval, damage to their sense of self-esteem or the loss of a sense of being lovable.

As the AT-T intervention neutralizes fear triggers it thereby diminishes the frequency of activation and intensity of the anger defense mechanism. But it is the sense of increased self-esteem, increased self-confidence and increased self-appreciation that motivates a teenager to continue with AT-T, whether via continued sessions with an AT-T psychotherapist or via self-application.

Psychotherapists need to recognize the connection between a client's perception of social and self-esteem threats and the spontaneous activation of the anger defense mechanism. They need to recognize the importance of neutralizing a client's perceived fear triggers in order to reduce the frequency and intensity of activation of their anger defense mechanism. Sadly, the "treatment" of serious anger problems is still anger management.

Most teenage delinquents have observed from early childhood that anger tends to be honored by adults in their family, by peers in their neighborhood, and by adults most everywhere. In fact, anger is probably the single most relied upon ego defense mechanism, regardless of age, education, occupation, or socioeconomic status. But it is especially honored and relied upon among criminally-, drug- and/or gang-oriented teenagers.

Therefore, it should not be surprising that teenage delinquents start out with serious doubts about the prospect of a therapy that enables them to rely less on their anger, in exchange for the vague sounding purpose of self-improvement, regardless of how eloquently it might be presented.

Substance Abuse

Historically, substances have been indulged in for the same reasons they are indulged in by today's teenage delinquents. Each substance has had the effect of temporarily sedating to some degree the threat of fear triggers. Even addictions to gambling, shopping, watching TV, or cleaning house have the effect of temporarily dulling one or more particular fears. While indulging in their addictive substance or activity of choice, the addict temporarily experiences less worry, less shame, less embarrassment, less hurt feelings, less grief, and so on.

To the degree that the substance or the activity has the intended effect of temporarily dulling their tendency to feel fear, then to that degree the addict is less troubled by thoughts associated with those fears. In the company of friends who are similarly under the influence of drugs, a teenager is essentially free of fear and free of fearful thoughts. To the AT-T psychotherapist this is not significantly different from the TV addict watching TV with a fellow TV addict, or a shopping addict going shopping with a fellow shopping addict, or a food addict going to a smorgasbord with another food addict.

It should not be cause for wonder that mutual bonding occurs among drug abusers. Mutual bonding can occur among individuals who are similarly addicted to an activity or pastime they can enjoy together. It should not be surprising that treating an addict who has the companionship of fellow addicts is more challenging than is treating an addict whose addiction behavior is such that it is acted out alone.

Most teenage drug users likely realize being under the influence temporarily reduces their worries about self-esteem and social status. Therefore, they tend to have reduced need for the anger defense mechanism and reduced need to be socially competitive. There are some interesting things of an esoteric or spiritual nature they could also experience, but the potential for anything like that is usually not noticed by the teenage drug abuser. Esoteric insights, if there is a potential in such cases, also goes unnoticed by the TV addict, the shopping addict, and the food addict.

Some Native Americans consider certain mind-altering substances—peyote, for instance—to be "sacred" because they associate their use—under the guidance of a spiritual leader, or medicine man—with the development of spiritual insight. Since spiritual insight cannot be measured, this remains scientifically un-researched. However, well educated non-Native Americans who have observed the tribal use of peyote for inducing spiritual insight have come away as impressed with that religious practice as with the practices of any world class religion. To participate in a ceremony involving peyote it is required that the individual understand the substance is considered sacred. At least one recognized peyote medicine man must be present and in charge of the ceremony. Native Americans who participate take the sacredness of a peyote ceremony quite seriously and expect to acquire some personally significant insight, which is then spiritually interpreted for them by the medicine man.

Substance abusers seldom have much grasp of ethical values, never use drugs under the guidance of any kind of spiritual mentor, and are interested primarily in peer approval and escape from their need to constantly scan for potential threats to their self-esteem and social status. As already mentioned, the major appeal of getting "high" is to partially sedate the ability to experience fear feelings. It seems obvious that the therapeutic neutralization of a teenage addict's perception of such threats should be a part of any treatment program.

In addition, if the most debilitating fear triggers have been identified and neutralized via AT-T, it follows that getting "high" to sedate the lesser fear triggers will be a less satisfying experience. For such a teenager, the appeal of ongoing drug use will have lost much of its appeal, and the prospect of sobriety less disappointing and saddening.

Sex Offenders

The sexual molestation of children is viewed by society as one of the most detestable of crimes. Yet, the damage done to victims of sexual abuse is seldom much worse than the non-sex related damage caused directly or indirectly to victims of parents who abuse alcohol or drugs. For that matter, many more children are caused much more emotional, psychological and physical damage due to poverty.

The psychotherapist needs to approach the treatment of clients with a history of sexual predation with the same practicality as with the treatment of any other client. The end of AT-T psychotherapy with a sex offender should be the significant reduction in the strength of his or her urges to re-offend, or hopefully, the total elimination of aberrant sexual urges.

The treatment of teenage sex offenders is complicated by the fact that their offenses involve a natural, strong urge to procreate—however distorted it might have become. The offender's normal sexual urges might have become distorted partly from having been reared in a severely dysfunctional family, from having viewed pornographic videos during early childhood, from the offender having been sexually molested, and/or from the offender's resentment due to a perception that a younger sibling—a common victim—received better treatment from the parents.

It is conceivable that the best form of therapy might be that which offers the best prospects of significantly improving the offender's self-esteem, if it is done via the neutralization of fear triggers that threaten self-esteem. The sex urge need not be eliminated, but as self-esteem is restored it follows that the offender might be less likely to experience an urge to sexually re-offend.

There is not a great deal that cognitive therapies can do about the fear and anger feelings associated with past hurtful events or those that are anticipated. But AT-T specifically addresses the fear and anger responses associated with past, present and imagined or anticipated future events. Restoration of a more normal sense of self-esteem would be the expected outcome. This might be about all that psychotherapy can do to rehabilitate the teenage sex offender, but it might be all that is needed. One might then expect maturity to develop the way it's supposed to, and the teenage offender to lose interest in re-offending, or even to wonder why sexually offending had seemed so appealing in the first place.

It has been understood for decades that aberrant behavior, whether it be drug abuse, alcohol abuse, stealing, violence, or sex offending, is anger-based. A great many psychotherapists understand that anger is fear-based. It is mystifying that most all treatment programs, whether for teenagers or adults, males or females, continue to rely almost exclusively on cognitive therapies and behavior modification. Year after year such programs struggle to achieve success rates higher than 25-30%, and year after year they fail to do so.

In addition, much of their so-called success rate with teenage offenders can be attributed to the successful onset of maturity, and the self-motivated decision to stop committing their offenses. In the case of adult offenders, much of their equally dismal "success" rate can be attributed to what is usually referred to as "burn out." This term refers to the fact that some middle-aged offenders finally decide they don't want to risk facing the consequences again of being caught. The sad truth is that most treatment programs, whether for teenage offenders or adult offenders, cannot truthfully take very much credit even for their meager success rates.

The teenager released from a correctional treatment program will usually have endured the one-size-fits-all cognitive treatment program whether it was needed or not. There will have been little or no therapeutic treatment to effectively address the fear and anger emotions that generate, and then reinforce, their delinquent values and their association with delinquent peers. The teenager is expected to refrain from sexually re-offending, relapsing into substance abuse, re-uniting with delinquent peers, or from further criminal activity by "remembering" the principles and the thinking techniques from the cognitive training. I don't know how to make the limitations of cognitive treatment any clearer!

References

Achterberg, Jeane (1985), *Imagery In Healing: Shamanism and Modern Medicine*, New Science Library, Shambala Publications, Inc., Boston, Massachusetts.

Amen, Daniel G. (1998), *Change Your Brain Change Your Life*, Three Rivers Press, New York.

Amen, Daniel G. (2001), *Healing ADD*, Berkeley Publishing Group, New York.

Carter, Rita (1998), *Mapping the Mind*, University of California Press, Berkeley, California.

Hallowell, Edward G., M.D. & Ratey, John J., M.D., (1994), *Driven To Distraction*, Simon & Schuster, New York.

Kelly, Kate & Ramundo, Peggy (1993), *You Mean I'm Not Lazy, Stupid Or Crazy?!* Tyrell & Jerem Press, Cincinnati, Ohio.

Keyes, Ken (1974), *The Handbook to Higher Consciousness*, Living Love Center, Berkeley, California.

Keyes, Ken (1979), *The Conscious Person's Guide to Relationships*, Living Love Publications; distributed by De Vorss, Berkeley, California.

Parnell, Laurel, Ph.D. (1997), *Transforming Trauma: EMDR*, W. W. Norton & Company, New York.

Ratey, John J., M.D., (2001), *A User's Guide to the Brain*, Pantheon Books, New York.

Shapiro, Francine, Ph.D. & Forrest, Margot Silk (1997), *EMDR*, Basic Books, The Perseus Books Group, New York.

Sheikh, Anees A., (1984), *Imagination and Healing*, Baywood Publishing Company, Inc., Farmingdale, New York.